ENDOF

"If you're yearning to be a part of something greater than yourself and to interact with the Father in an intimate way, your search stops here. *Praying for Reign* is like a master class on God's design for prayer and His personal invitation for you to join Him. Don's wisdom and revelation will leave you equipped and hungry to embark on a great adventure with the Father. With a fresh perspective and new revelation, you'll begin to seek the Lord with expectancy and boldness, knowing the part you play in His grand story. Rich in truth and biblical revelation, this is a book sure to stand the test of time and inspire generations to seek the heart of God for their personal role in Praying for Reign."

— Ashlee Kasten, pastoral leader of the Focus Church (Apex Campus) in North Carolina, and the author of *Because She Prayed* and *Lessons I Learned in The Laundry Basket.*

"Prayer is the way we write history before it happens! This book will help you do just that."

—Dr. Mark Batterson, Head Pastor of National Community Church and New York Times bestselling author of more than twenty books.

"This is a powerful book Don has written. The stories that he shares will not only inspire you, but they will also show you how important it is to pray. *Praying for Reign* will encourage you that prayer does indeed work."

— Pastor Rick Van Wagner, Senior Pastor at Family Christian Center in Central Florida.

"I was blessed to preview *Praying for Reign* before its release and literally could not stop reading it once I started. Powerful enlightenment of profound, life-changing principles."

— Coach Randy Pippin, Director of Player Development at University of Alabama at Birmingham, thirty-plus year veteran college football coach, and author of *Deep in the Heart*.

———•———

"Does prayer really work? Maybe the better question is: 'Do we believe prayer works?' For every person navigating this question, Don Newman's masterpiece, *Praying for Reign*, opens a well of revelation on the power of prayer that will send you to your knees!

Praying for Reign builds faith to pray. *Praying for Reign* develops the language of breakthrough in prayer. *Praying for Reign* restores hope in the discipline of praying.

Praying for Reign is quite simply the new field manual for the believing church as its warring for divine recovery!"

— Kevin Craig, Senior Pastor at Thrive Church in Apopka, Florida.

———•———

"A.W. Tozer once preached a message entitled 'In Everything By Prayer,' which impacted me as I did my time working with Evangelist Reinhard Bonnke—who was a man of intense prayer. The Puritan Pilgrims were people whose entire foundational truths came from a baptism of prayer. The apostolic epoch that we are now entering is the fulfillment of the desire of Jesus, that His church would be a house of prayer for all nations.

This is not the mere amplification of prayer as it is often perceived. It is not the addition of a missing prayer component, or prayer even as a bountiful additive, a power-pack, to what we are currently doing. It is not the mere deepening or heightening of the value of prayer. It is a seismic apostolic shift.

Herein in *Praying for Reign*, Don Newman reminds us of the history of how the Holy Spirit births everything in and through prayer. To be used as a vessel of intercession is a high calling. In a heaven-to-earth work of a superintending Holy Spirit, our God chooses to work through His remnant body to come into agreement for His perfect will to be administered in the earth."

— Rev. Kevin Jessip, Co-Chair of The Return and President of Global Strategic Alliance.

"The disciples asked Jesus, 'Teach us to pray.' Their proximity to our Savior had given them a front-row seat to His devotional life. They noticed that when Jesus prayed, Heaven moved. They desired to do likewise. Today, hungry Christ-followers are still asking the same question. They long to pierce the heavens with their intercession and move mountains with their prayers.

I believe *Praying for Reign* has come into your hands at just the right moment. You will find it to be a stone upon which you can sharpen your sword and experience a more effective and rewarding prayer life. There is certainly no higher call than to partner with God in prayer and see His plan accomplished on earth as it is in Heaven. Don is a spiritual marksman and a true intercessor. His life and longevity in ministry mean his words can be trusted as this message has been battle-tested."

— Daniel K. Norris, author, evangelist, and Lead Pastor at Grace World Outreach Church in Brooksville, Florida.

"In *Praying for Reign*, Don Newman equips and empowers the prayer warrior in executing the mandates of praying 'Thy kingdom come' through prayer. God's original mandate 'to take dominion over the earth' in Genesis can be realized through effective prayer that accomplishes much! This is not your typical book on prayer. You must read it and then act upon what you learn."

— Dr. Larry Keefauver, bestselling author of more than sixty books and international teacher.

"Don Newman has a unique way of writing that helps the reader 'see' what he's saying and understand as if he is talking to you in person. His new book *Praying for Reign* helps us understand the position of partnering with God through prayer to see His plan for manifesting His kingdom realm here as it is in Heaven. He gives us tools for effective prayer and revelations from Jesus about how to do this and why it's important.

This book will give you great insight and help you mature in your intimacy with Jesus as you learn to pray His will, and do it His way."

— Mary Kemp-Smith, Senior Co-Pastor
of New Life Church in Houston, Texas.

"It has been said that prayer has two dimensions: a heart-to-heart connection of intimacy with God, and a shoulder-to-shoulder co-laboring with Him to build His kingdom on earth as it is in Heaven. In *Praying for Reign*, Don Newman gives both encouragement and specific guidance to all who yearn for their lives to grow in both of these dimensions. In a wonderfully solid, biblical way, Don pulls from his own experience as well as church history to both instruct and inspire us to pick up our 'swords and shields' of prayer to fulfill God's eternal designs for His church.

I heartily commend this book to you as you put both heart and shoulder into a more flourishing life of prayer."

— Dr. Bob Mitchell, author of *The Giant David Could Not Kill* and
Pastor at Idyllwild Community Church
in Idyllwild California.

"Prayer played such a huge role in the life and story of every person in scripture who was called of God. Jesus demonstrated such a consistent life of reigning prayer, as well as the early church, and experienced supernatural signs, wonders, solutions, and multiplication all for the glory of God. This is what we long for in our generations! *Praying for Reign* is such an important encouragement and reminder to God's people of the powerful weapon we have been given and the authority we have when we pray in Christ's name to see Heaven come! You will love reading Don's stories, as they stir you to prayer and inspire you to partner with God in new ways to see Heaven manifested in every area of your life! "

— Kent Mattox, Pastor at Word Alive International Outreach.

Praying
FOR Reign

NEVER UNDERESTIMATE THE POWER

AND IMPACT OF YOUR PRAYERS

DON NEWMAN

XULON PRESS

Xulon Press
2301 Lucien Way #415
Maitland, FL 32751
407.339.4217
www.xulonpress.com

Paperback ISBN-13: 978-1-66282-817-1
Dust Jacket ISBN-13: 978-1-66286-592-3
Ebook ISBN-13: 978-1-66282-818-8

TABLE OF CONTENTS

ACKNOWLEDGEMENTS

Learning and living out the practice of prayer has been the greatest adventure of my life, but it has not been alone. Many people have been part of this journey with me, both past and present. I simply would not know the incredible truths I have learned about prayer without the influence of many other people.

The first person I want to thank is my wife, Tracee. She has not only supported me through my journey of learning and writing on prayer, she has also been one of the greatest living examples I have learned from. Year after year I watched her pray, and like the disciples did with Jesus, I learned the power of prayer from watching her quiet but meaningful prayer life. She not only is my greatest partner in prayer, she has also been my teacher, even if she never realized it.

I want to also acknowledge my children and their spouses, and my grandchildren. Your lives have been one of my greatest assignments for prayer. I learned much about prayer through praying for all of you, but your support for both my writing and ministry has made all the difference.

To my future descendants. Know that I have prayed for you and my prayer is that this book influences your walk with Christ and your prayer life.

Special thanks to my daughter Brittnee, who is not just my editor but really, she is my co-writer. Thank you, Britt.

My great-aunt, Epsie McKay. There is nothing like a generational mantle for prayer, and I am thankful that I walk in hers. While she never actually gave it to me, I know that God did. I want to encourage every reader to realize that their prayers do not only influence the current generation, they also influence future generations. Aunt Epsie's prayer life continues on because it influenced mine and now it lives on through this book to influence many more generations.

I must also thank Dutch Sheets, Chuck Pierce, Ken Malone, Mark Batterson, Cindy Jacobs, and Rebecca Greenwood. You and the ministries you lead have provided revelation, leadership, and direction to me and many more like me. There is an army that is falling in behind the work you have started. Thank you for leading the way in prayer. May any fruit from my own teaching be multiplied back to each of you for the part you have played for helping to lead the prayer movement.

Finally, I must thank my team at Xulon that worked so hard at getting this project finished. On that team are three key people who played the biggest part of making this book a reality. That trio of superstars begins with Amanda Wright, who designed the amazing cover for *Praying for Reign*. Also in that group were Melinda Howard and Kim Small, who both worked with me on the interior design and layout. Outside of those three there were about a dozen coworkers who helped to proof the final manuscript before it went to print. I am extremely blessed to work with and help lead such an amazing team. They truly are the best!

INTRODUCTION

What if you knew it was going to be *your* prayers that transformed your entire family? What if your prayers are the ones God needs to move a child or family member into a relationship with Christ? How would you feel about prayer if you found out that your prayers were the tipping point for moving America into a revival? Would that change how you felt about prayer, and the part you play? I believe the answer would be yes.

Unfortunately, most Christians underestimate the power of their prayers. In truth, we underestimate the power of prayer because we simply underestimate ourselves. We doubt that God could use our five or ten minutes of petition because we can't imagine that the prayers of one person out of eight billion people could have that much pull. We'd all like to think our prayers matter that much, but it can be hard to accept if we are focused on our own frailties and mistakes.

Prayer never fails, but we fail to pray. The main reasons are either we think we are too insignificant, or we are too unworthy to call Heaven down to earth. Let me assure you, nothing could be further from the truth. If you are a Christian, God has not only called you to pray, He has also equipped you to pray. We have been empowered to make a real difference in this world through prayer. In fact, God is depending on us to pray: to Pray for Reign.

THE SATURDAY WHEN EVERYTHING CHANGED

Every story has its beginning. While I did pray growing up, my prayers seemed to be one-dimensional at best. Over the years that changed as I began to understand that prayer was much more than just asking God for things; it was about a relationship. My growth as a Christian and as an intercessor led me down many paths to learning about prayer, but nothing changed my view like the encounter I had with the Lord one Saturday morning. On this day it was like God opened the door to His royal treasury, allowing me to see things I'd never seen before.

On that Saturday morning, I sat in my office praying and asked the Lord, "What are the keys to revival? How should I pray to see real change?" The condition of America was weighing heavily upon me, and I really was seeking direction on how I should pray. It was urgent, but I was not in any hurry. I sipped my coffee and just listened for His voice. This was not the first time I'd asked that question of the Lord, as praying for revival and awakening is an almost-daily conversation I have with Him. But this day was different; this day shifted my understanding of prayer into a whole new dimension.

THREE EMPTY BOATS

As I drank my coffee and listened in the quiet for God to answer me, I heard the Holy Spirit tell me to look up at the paintings located just above my bookcase. On the wall hung three acrylic paintings of three separate sailboats. The boats were not anything special or unique; just decorative art that give my home office a nautical feel. As I peered at them while still thinking about America's critical need for an awakening, I got the immediate impression that the answer to my question was hidden somewhere in these paintings. God can speak to us through anything He chooses, and on this day, He was speaking through three boats.

As I analyzed the boats for some thread of commonality, I thought, *Well, they are all in a harbor, so that's not it.* Then I thought, *Well, they are all red and white in color.* Still, nothing seemed to click. It did not come all at once, but I finally recognized what these three boats had in common. All three boats were empty; there was no one on board any of the boats. I could feel the peace of God run through me, confirming that I was on the right track. I knew my answer had something to do with the fact these boats were unmanned.

While it was great to know that I was beginning to hear God through these three paintings, I needed to understand how they related to praying for an awakening in America. When I think "boats," I always think "fishing." I grew up fishing with my dad and brother in a little jon boat we would take out on the lake. Later in life, I bought a larger boat that I would use to fish the many ponds and lakes in North Florida. There was nothing like being out on the water on a sunny day, catching fish.

In the Bible, catching fish is used to illustrate both harvest and soul-winning. Everyone knows the story in Luke chapter five; the one where Jesus directs Peter to go back out and cast his net one more time. In this story, Peter was at first reluctant because they had already fished and had caught nothing, but in the end, he did as Jesus asked. The result was that they caught such a great number of fish that their net started to break. They even had to ask for help from others to get the full catch ashore. What an amazing story!

Hidden within that story and the paintings on my wall was a powerful truth God was trying to teach me about prayer, but first He had to talk to me about boats. As I sipped my coffee and listened, I heard this: "This *true miracle* of catching fish would never have happened if no one was in that boat. If Peter and his friends were on the shore, it would have never happened." As I continued to pray and consider the revelation I just received, it became crystal clear to me: God will not work through unmanned boats. He needs someone on the boat to work through. In the big picture, God needs someone on this side of Heaven to play their part in order for Him to fulfill His part.

Because I was talking about God, it seemed difficult to say "He needed." Saying God needs anything just goes against the idea that He can do anything—but what if He set it up that way? What if God wanted His work on earth to be dependent upon the obedience and participation of His children? What if God, in His infinite wisdom, placed us in a position that holds the keys to His plan on earth?

You might be asking what "Praying for Reign" is. First, it is both the act of actively partnering with God, *and* the act of agreeing with God in prayer. What are we partnering and agreeing on? The fulfillment of His plan: His plan to manifest His kingdom realm on earth as it is in Heaven. It's a bit lengthy, but when we put that all together it's this: Praying for Reign is partnering and agreeing with God through prayer for the fulfillment of His plan—His plan to manifest His kingdom realm on earth as it is in Heaven.

God designed prayer not just as a way to commune with Him, but also a way to partner with Him in His work. To follow up on the word picture we discussed earlier, prayer is manning the boats so He can direct us and use us to catch the fish. Remember, God cannot use unmanned boats to produce a catch. He needs us to get in the boat, pray in the fish, and ask Him to send others to help us. He needs us to pray.

PRAYING FOR REIGN

Where can you Pray for Reign? Anywhere God calls you to! But in this book, I focus on four key areas:

- You can Pray for Reign in the church.
- You can Pray for Reign in your job.
- You can Pray for Reign in your family.
- You can Pray for Reign in America.

Imagine: through partnering with God through prayer, you have the ability to see God's presence and kingdom manifested in your church, your job, your family, and all of America. In the end, nothing is exempt from the power of His kingdom when a believer plays their part and prays. That person could be you. You could be the person God uses to create an awakening where you work. You also could be the catalyst for God moving in your church and eventually the community.

In this book, you will learn how God is not only commanding us to pray, He really is inviting us to pray. Inviting us as His children to partner with Him in establishing and expanding His kingdom. Throughout the book, you will hear three things repeated several times:

1. Prayer is more about God getting our attention than us getting His.
2. God does nothing except through prayer.
3. God does not want us to do things for Him as much as He wants us to do things with Him. Prayer is a partnership, not a performance. Prayer is participating in the family business of God.

These truths are important to understand as you learn how to Pray for Reign. I encourage you to ask the Holy Spirit to guide you and teach you as you read through this book. The Holy Spirit is our greatest prayer partner, and no one can instruct us like He can. God has given us everything we need to partner with Him as He manifests His kingdom on earth as in Heaven.

If you are reading this book, know that I have prayed for you, that God through His Holy Spirit would teach you how to Pray for Reign. I believe God is going to use my prayer for you. I believe both Jesus and the Holy Spirit are interceding for you as well. You are not alone and you are not insignificant; you are significant enough that He is actually counting on you to pray. Who knows what God may use you to do for His kingdom when you learn how to Pray for Reign?

Let's find out together, shall we?

SECTION ONE

THY KINGDOM COME

The Power and Purpose of Praying for Reign

Chapter One

GOD WANTS YOU TO PRAY FOR REIGN

Discovering How Your Prayers Really Matter

In a land far, far away...

I have always loved epic tales that showcase the battle of good versus evil. Stories where the odds are not necessarily with the hero or heroine, but are stacked against them—and despite the odds, they overcome and experience great victory no one could have projected or expected.

Hollywood is famous for writing stories just like this; ones that push movie-goers to the edge of their seat, blindly pushing popcorn into their mouth as they watch the plot build to its climax. No one, however, has written more stories of triumph than God Himself. Through His power, there have been untold stories that have been lived out by those who know Him and know the power of His kingdom. What you may not have realized is God wants you to play a starring role in the epic stories He composes. He wants you to Pray for Reign. You may ask, "What part could I play?" That is why this book was written: to call your attention to the part only you can play, and show you how important that part really is—specifically through prayer.

Do you realize your prayers can bring the kingdom of Heaven to earth? Or do you feel your prayers are just part of the mist that forms into droplets and eventually produces rain? Yes, that mist is important, but it's so easy to feel like it's so tiny, so unimportant that is easily replaceable and made up by someone else. The plan and lie of the enemy is clear: make every Christian feel like their own prayers are so insignificant that no one prays.

> **The plan and lie of the enemy is clear: make every Christian feel like their own prayers are so insignificant that no one prays.**

Praying for Reign is partnering and agreeing with God through prayer for the fulfillment of His plan—His plan to manifest His kingdom realm on earth as it is in Heaven. The reason your prayers matter—even if you are the only one praying—is because you are partnering with God. As you Pray for Reign, you cooperate with what God initiates so you are not praying alone; you are praying with and partnering with God. You + God will always equal a majority. At various points in history, the world has been changed by one man or one woman who believed this principle and made the decision to partner with God in prayer.

In this book, you will find an open invitation for you to join God in the incredible work that He is continuing today. The amazing part is that if you will accept it, you already have a part to play and a unique role written just for you. As we look throughout history, we can find others who played their role in the prequel to our story, and participated in some of the greatest acts of all time. Acts that just happened to intersect with their life's trajectory, but when presented with the opportunity to participate in His grand plan, they heard God and partnered with Him.

> **Praying for Reign is partnering and agreeing with God through prayer for the fulfillment of His plan—His plan to manifest His kingdom realm on earth as it is in Heaven.**

While I don't think anything happens randomly, the most important question for us to answer is this: what will intersect with your lifetime that is your uniquely appointed opportunity to make a difference for the kingdom of God? This is what Praying for Reign is all about. It's understanding that we were created and born again by the Spirit to fulfill the purposes of God in the earth during this time.

For example, you may ask, "Why did the coronavirus have to come in my lifetime?" A better question would be "Heavenly Father, why am I alive during this present crisis and what am I to do about it?" When we begin to understand the pre-designed role that we have been called to play in God's incredible story and in His ever-expanding and eternal kingdom, we begin to understand we were placed here during this time for a specific purpose. Yes, as followers of Christ we are called to make a difference in the world during the time we live in.

> **"God does nothing except in response to believing prayer."**
> **John Wesley**

While action is always needed in times of difficulty, we must learn that nothing makes a difference like prayer. In the words of John Wesley, "God does nothing except in response to believing prayer." God has called you and I to pray, but it's important to understand not only the purpose of that prayer, but also the power that stands behind it.

In hindsight of a miracle, the cynic will always try to tell you that prayer did nothing and those things would have occurred on their own, with or without prayer. The cynic is not only wrong, they are also sadly deceived. If they only understood that, for the believer, prayer is like receiving a key to a gate that guards not only the very answer we are in need of, but one that has also been planned and purposed by God. If they only understood that God in His Sovereignty set up this system so that we would not just be spectators, but actual participants with Him in His mighty plan of redemption. While it's true that we could never redeem or save ourselves, God calls us to participate with Him and play our part in its unfolding. God doesn't just call us to pray *to* Him, but to pray *with* Him as He builds His kingdom.

While there are many stories to illustrate how men and women have partnered with God in prayer, one of my favorites takes place during the dark days of WWII. We will never know all of the answers to prayer that came during that "war to end all wars," but I guarantee you that they are too numerous to count. This act unfolded during one of the darkest days of the war when it looked like England would surely be overrun by the evil forces of Nazi Germany. This story is often referred to as the Miracle of Dunkirk.[2]

THE MIRACLE OF DUNKIRK: PRAYING FOR REIGN IN WORLD WAR II

Over eighty years ago, something happened that would baffle the minds of both the great and the weak. It was so incredible that it was called a miracle, an act of God; something no man could ever create on their own. In the end, all anyone could do was just participate in it and thank God for it.

> God doesn't just call us to pray *to* Him, but to pray *with* Him as He builds His kingdom.

The year was 1940 and the United Kingdom was fully entrenched in a war with Germany; one that would eventually include America. For England, they had entered this war in hopes that it would end all wars. On September 3, 1939, England and France declared war on Germany in response to Germany's invasion of Poland.

Less than a year later, the citizens of Great Britain faced one of the darkest days of their long existence as a country. Just over twenty miles from their own coastline, a battle raged that would most likely determine if they would remain free or come under the control of an evil and brutal leader seeking world domination. It was in a place in Northern France called Dunkirk where these allied forces found themselves trapped like sitting ducks, with the English Channel on one side and the advancing German Army on the other. Defeat and tyranny stood and sneered from mere miles away, and the only thing separating them from this certain outcome was the prayers of Christians, and the heroic efforts of brave citizens willing to use their personal boats to cross the English Channel and ferry trapped soldiers to England.

It would have been one thing if the odds of this battle were in their favor, but even the German military leaders knew there was no way this retreating army had any chance against the air and land attack they were about to execute. This was truly a "red sea moment" for England, and just as in Exodus, a miracle from God was the only hope of avoiding destruction. In the end, there really was no chance of victory, only desperate hopes of escape. German High Command issued a global statement that the British army was totally surrounded, and the German troops were advancing to annihilate them.

News that the British Army in France was facing total destruction sent shockwaves through the country and the leadership of Great Britain. Outside of a Plan B or a miracle, Prime Minister Winston Churchill would have to inform the nation that over a third of their army had been captured or killed. While the loss itself would be great, what would most likely come next would be even worse. Without that strategically placed outpost to defend against an advancing German Army, invasion of England would certainly be next. While we can speculate on the consequences of that invasion, it is most likely that Germany would have gone on to control Europe—and who knows what else.

Have you ever faced a serious situation where all seems lost if God does not step in? Nothing can turn a person or nation toward God like knowing that without His aid, there is no hope. While God wants us to understand that we can and should come to Him in prayer in times of extreme need, it's equally important to join Him in prayer in times of apparent peace. It's during those lulls or times of inactivity, when we continue to pray, that God prepares us for the future battles we will face.

England knew this was dire and even the leadership of that day saw the need to call on God for help. King George VI requested on May 23 that the following Sunday be observed as a National Day of Prayer. In a powerful scene documented for history, the nation turned out to pray all across Great Britain. The people were stepping up to help the trapped military the only way they knew how: to appeal to Heaven.

Eventually, England made a decision to use their military to remove as many soldiers from the beaches of Dunkirk as possible, in what was called "Operation Dynamo." It soon became clear that would not be enough. They realized they would need the help of every person who had a boat to make the journey across the English Channel to rescue soldiers, and make it back again safely. To do this in a time when the German Luftwaffe had planes flying all over the area, and given the difficulty of the crossing itself due to difficult weather and the possibility of a passing German U-boat, this would require more than the help of brave men. It would require the help of God.

GOD STEPS IN

Have you ever wondered how God can answer our prayers even before we even pray them? I personally believe it's because God-birthed prayers live in eternal spaces and are not limited to time as we understand it. I believe that God knew well beforehand that Germany would not only invade Poland, but would also overrun the forces in Belgium to trap the allied forces in a place called Dunkirk. God was not taken aback by this or surprised, but He needed someone to stand in the gap and ask Him to step in. What happened next can only be explained as not just one miracle, but three.

Miracle Number One: Hitler stops the advance. At almost the same time that King George VI called for national prayer, Hitler unexpectedly called for his advancing army to stop. Imagine: the allies are trapped like sitting ducks, and the leader of the advancing army tells his army to stop with certain victory just a few miles away. It is recorded that Hitler's generals became upset, and why wouldn't they? They had fought this far and the eventual victory of the war was only a few miles away. In the natural realm, they should have kept advancing, but something caused Hitler to command them to stop and stay idle for three days. It was those three days that provided the time for the small boats to prepare and make the trip to start the rescue. No one knows what made Hitler stop, although there is a lot of speculation from those who don't believe in miracles. In the end, it may not have been seen by the eyes of man or Hitler himself, but there was an Exodus-like "pillar of fire," holding his army back.

Miracle Number Two: The planes were grounded. The weather grounded the German Luftwaffe at their airfield in Flanders. Even though the German Army had stopped advancing, they still had plans to send their planes to attack the retreating allied soldiers. One can only imagine the demise of so many brave men as plane after plane shot at them on the ground and bombed any location they sought cover in. This bad weather not only protected the allies from attack, it allowed the soldiers who were still retreating to move toward the beaches where their eventual escape would be secured.

Miracle Number Three: The English Channel was calm. While the weather was bad enough to keep most of the planes grounded in France, it was calm enough to the west to make the English Channel as still as a mill pond, making it easier for the small boats to cross over. The large ships could only enter from one point to pick the soldiers up. In the end, it was the little boats that joined the rescue which made all the difference. Over eight hundred and fifty private boats and yachts responded to the call for help and made the journey through the channel to rescue the allied soldiers trapped at Dunkirk. The smooth waters of the English Channel helped them make the crossing in the narrow window of time they had.

Two of the three miracles were clearly miracles involving weather. While only God controls the weather, we know from the story of Elijah and his encounters with King Ahab that God will use a man or woman to initiate those miracles through prayer.

> The effective, fervent prayer of a righteous man avails much. Elijah was a man with a nature like ours, and he prayed earnestly that it would not rain; and it did not rain on the land for three years and six months. And he prayed again, and the heaven gave rain, and the earth produced its fruit. James 5:16b-18

There is no doubt that the prayers of the citizens who responded to King George's call to prayer had been heard and God intervened, avoiding a larger disaster, likely German invasion, and occupation of Great Britain.

I'm confident there were key intercessors who were already praying ahead of this event, not only influencing the war, but possibly influencing leaders like King George and Winston Churchill through their prayers. Many times, the men and women whom God uses to Pray for Reign and to influence the world are not seen—at least not while they are living. Many are hidden until later on when their stories are told for thousands. I truly believe there were great men and women of prayer during that dark time praying for their country and also for their leaders and king. One of those great intercessors who had an influence on the affairs of the war, the government, and King George was a man named Rees Howells.

Many times, the men and women whom God uses to Pray for Reign and to influence the world are not seen—at least not while they are living. Many are hidden until later on when their stories are told for thousands.

REES HOWELLS:
ONE MAN WHO MADE A DIFFERENCE
THROUGH PRAYER

You may have already known the story of King George VI and how he called the country to prayer in its darkest hour, but very few people know the true story about a man of God who lived about one hundred and eighty five miles west of London, a man seen as a key player in partnering with God in intercession regarding the war. Like so many other intercessors of that time, this hidden warrior and the company of prayer warriors he led were praying against the forces of evil seeking to overtake the world and stop the spread of the Gospel of Christ. The story of Rees Howells and the Bible College of Wales[1] he led is amazing and a must-learn for anyone who wants to understand what it means to be called as an intercessor.

Howells was the founder and head of the Bible College of Wales, which he started in the City of Swansea on the Southern Coast of Wales in 1924.[1] Called to be an intercessor, Rees Howells was part of a great revival in South Africa in the early twentieth century. His life taught us that there is a marked difference between someone who is called to be a prayer warrior and someone called to be an intercessor. According to Rees, prayer warriors are so valuable in moving God's hand, but they are able to pray and then leave when they are done praying. Intercessors are more rare. They, unlike prayer warriors, cannot leave when they are done praying; they can only leave when it is finished. The life of an intercessor is truly a life of sacrifice.

In the book *Rees Howells, Intercessor,* written by Norman Grub,[2] you can read about Howells' life and how he was not only called to intercede for the purposes of God, but also to lead others into prayer. It's the portions of the book that detail his intercession during the years of WWII that moved me deeply and revealed to me how I could make a difference through prayer and intercession. In the end, God is no respecter of persons, and He can use anyone who is willing to say yes the same way He used Howells. I love to think that someone reading this book may go on to become another Rees Howells.

IT STARTED WITH A VISON

To give you a little insight into this powerful man and leader of prayer, several years prior to the Miracle of Dunkirk, Rees Howells received a vison from God in which God gave him direction to pray for the completion of the Great Commission, that every person would hear and understand the Gospel of Christ.

As WWII began and the rise of evil dictators saw Hitler, Stalin, and Mussolini come on the scene, Rees saw this Axis of Evil becoming the biggest threat to not just Britain, but also the spread of the Gospel of the kingdom of God. These leaders were obviously an enemy set against freedom and the spread of Christianity. The growing wave of darkness in Europe caused Rees to ask God for direction on how he should pray. He needed to know what to pray in order to stop this evil so that the Gospel could go to the whole world. Praying for Reign will always be connected to God's plan to expand His kingdom through the furtherance of the Gospel of Christ. That is the ultimate endgame of Praying for Reign.

> **Praying for Reign will always be connected to God's plan to expand His kingdom through the furtherance of the Gospel of Christ. That is the ultimate endgame of Praying for Reign.**

When we are directed by God to pray that the dark gates of a foreign country are opened for the work of God to penetrate, we are not just praying for unhindered travel, we are also praying that the Gospel would be unhindered in that region. When we are directed by God to pray for the election of godly leaders on our local school board, it's not just for the policies to match our political opinions, it's also so that the Gospel can penetrate that school district.

The key word is "directed." When we are directed by God to partner with Him in prayer regarding a situation, whether it be by His Word or by His Spirit, that is when we are Praying for Reign. The Lord's Prayer (which will be broken down later in this book) is one of the greatest guides for Praying for Reign. In it we are given specific direction from the greatest intercessor ever, our Lord Jesus Christ. When He tells us to pray, "Your kingdom come, Your will be done, On earth as *it is* in heaven," (Matt. 6:10), this was not just a suggestion, but divine direction.

When Rees Howells and the students of the Bible College would gather in what they called "The Blue Room" to pray, they were not just praying the prayers of their own heart's desire. True, like everyone else they wanted to see the war end and evil dictators defeated, but their prayers originated from higher than just their own fears and desires, they originated from the supreme commander of the universe. That is what Praying for Reign is all about, and if you are a follower of Christ, you are being invited to participate just as Rees was invited. While most of us will never carry the burden for prayer that Rees Howells had, we all still have a strategic place to fill.

WHAT WALES TAUGHT ME

As a young intercessor and one who was called to prayer, I have read this incredible story of Rees Howells numerous times, but I have also traveled to Wales and visited the Bible College myself. I have stood in the very room where Howells and his students would pray for hours a day, asking God to intervene and defeat the evil armies who sought to conquer England, Europe, and much of the free world. What is so amazing to me is that God would actually show him outcomes and what to pray for. It was as though he and his students were in an underground war bunker drawing the maps for the upcoming battles. Their job was to agree with God in prayer for what He was showing them and persevere in prayer until it was finished.

To understand their resolve and their influence upon the outcome of the war is to understand the place we can all step into if we will answer the call to Pray for Reign. To Rees Howells, it was the job of he and his students to win the battle in prayer so the army could win the battle on land, sea, and air.

Can one man who prays make a difference in the world? Can someone who is hidden from public view have an influence in the seen world? Rees Howells' life and testimony answers with an astounding yes, God wants you to pray!

He not only wants you to pray, but more importantly, He wants you to pray in agreement with Him. God wants you to Pray for Reign.

> To Rees Howells, it was the job of he and his students to win the battle in prayer so the army could win the battle on land, sea, and air.

If you don't already know this, it's time for you to understand that your prayers not only count, but more importantly, that God is counting on them. I repeat, God is counting on your prayers.

Chapter Two

MONSTERS AND GIRLFRIENDS

Where Prayer Begins (But Doesn't End)

All learning has a beginning. We start somewhere, but that's not where we end up. Before you learned to ride a motorcycle, you probably learned to ride a bike. Before you learned how to scuba dive, you surely must have learned how to swim. I played baseball when I was younger, but it all began with a ball sitting on a tee.

While there are not necessarily "levels of prayer," it does make for a good illustration to help each of you know and understand this: God not only wants you to pray, He wants you to pray with increasing understanding and power. He wants you to grow in prayer and learn how to Pray for Reign.

When I was young, I prayed a lot, particularly about things I wanted or things I was scared of. I like to say I was praying to repel monsters and

> God not only wants you to pray, He wants you to pray with increasing understanding and power.

draw girlfriends—well, at least the ones I liked. Being a young Christian, I knew God was real and I knew that I could pray for things that were beyond my control or my own natural abilities. Early on in my life, I gained a fascination about the supernatural, especially when it came to things of God. I remember listening to people talk about angels and it created a holy fascination in me. Were they really real, and could I see one? One of my favorite books was *Angels* by Billy Graham.

BREAKING THE GLASS OF EMERGENCY PRAYER

Even with my young and deepening desire to know God and peek into the realms of the supernatural, I was just a red-blooded American boy who loved hunting and playing football. Many times, I think I just felt like I had it all—outside of the kind of troubles everyone has–and that I was good. Prayer was for when I *needed* it, as if prayer was tucked behind a glass door that read, "Break Only In Case Of Emergency."

While I reserved prayer for emergencies only, I can tell you there were a few times I needed to break that glass. One of those was when, for some unknown reason, I started losing weight because my food was basically just going straight through my body without being digested. I will spare you the details, but I went from one-hundred-and-eighty pounds to about one-hundred-and-thirty in a matter of a few months.

> Prayer was for when I *needed* it, as if prayer was tucked behind a glass door that read, "Break Only In Case Of Emergency."

The doctors could not find out what it was, and although they tested everything (and I mean everything), they said the next step was to put me in the hospital and feed me intravenously. Both I and the situation were looking very bad. I will never forget the night when my praying mom had me and my dad get on our knees with her and pray for God to heal me. I mean, if doctors can't do anything then what choice do you have? It was time to break the glass and start praying. Miraculously, everything changed the very next day. Again, not to be too descriptive, but there is nothing like calling your family to the bathroom to see that you were healed. I don't think anyone cares about what people think when God shows up.

I remember another time when I was young and I thought I had cancer. It sounds crazy, but all you need to do is find a bump and the rest is history...and this was before we could search on Google. I don't know if I overheard something that started the notion; all I know is I was convinced I had it, even though my dad said, "Don't be silly, you don't have cancer; you're fine." I can remember working to believe and trust my dad because my dad never lied; he was absolutely trustworthy. I remember battling the fear and opening my green-covered Living Bible to Psalm 23. This became my "break glass" scripture.

> Because the Lord is my Shepherd, I have everything I need! He lets me rest in the meadow grass and leads me beside the quiet streams. He gives me new strength. He helps me do what honors him the most. Even when walking through the dark valley of death I will not be afraid, for you are close beside me, guarding, guiding all the way. Psalm 23:1-4, TLB

As I read the scripture by the light of my "cowboy" lamp, I remember talking to God in my head and pouring out my heart to Him, asking Him to help me, to heal me. I didn't want to die and I was calling out for help. I remember many other times when I didn't go to sleep for hours as I wrestled in my bed between fear and prayer. It seemed I would shut my light off only to turn it back on again to grab my Bible to read that promise once again. While I am sure this was part of my spiritual journey—to learn how to reach out to the God of my parents—it was more of a starting place for prayer than a destination.

There are so many in the Body of Christ who started learning how to talk to God with prayers like:

"Now I lay me down to sleep. I pray the Lord my soul to keep. If I should die before I wake, I pray to God my soul to take."

PRAYING FOXHOLE PRAYERS

These early places of prayer for me almost always emerged from periods of extreme need or fear. Some people refer to them as "foxhole prayers." You may not recognize the name William Thomas Cummings, but you probably recognize a famous saying that has been attributed to him: "There are no atheists in foxholes." While there is no concrete evidence that Father Cummings said it, I could imagine it coming from someone like him. Lt. William Cummings served as a U.S. Army Chaplain to the American and Filipino soldiers who were battling against the Japanese Army in the Philippines. As you read historical accounts of the battle for the island, you understand what the term "foxhole prayers" means. While we might debate who actually coined the phrase, I think we agree that the foxholes of life produce prayers of all kinds.

Although I know my first prayers were not uttered on the edge of impending capture or death, they did feel desperate at times. I remember one time there was a girl whom I wanted to date really badly. I think I prayed, with tears, as I asked God to make a way for her to like me as much as I liked her. My poor little teenage heart was so consumed that all I could think about was her. All I will say today about this prayer is that the words of one of my favorite Garth Brooks songs make so much sense now. Trust me, I do thank God that He never answered that prayer. God had someone so much better for me than the girl I was praying for; He was reserving someone He had destined me to be with. I didn't know that back then, so I just poured out my young pleading heart to God because I knew He was real.

The wonderful thing about God is even when I was calling out to Him, mostly about myself, He was still there for me. He not only listened to me and brought peace into my life, but He also answered a few of those earlier prayers (though thankfully not the one about the girl I thought I could not live without!). Of all of the things I love about our God, I love that He loves me so much, that He taught me how to pray as a child. He knew I had to begin as a child to progress from a new believer to a spiritual son, from a servant to a friend, from a stranger to an heir. Prayer is a journey and where it begins is not where it ends—that is if you continue to grow and learn not only how to communicate with God, but also partner with Him in what He wants to do.

WHAT PRAYER IS NOT

When we begin our journey in prayer with God, we can have all kinds of wrong or misguided ideas. We might carry the following misconceptions:

- Prayer originates with us.
- Prayer is all about our needs, wants, and desires.
- Prayer is interrupting God or causing Him to stop what He is doing.
- Prayer is trying to convince God of something by twisting His arm.
- Prayer should sound religious to be accepted or useful.
- Prayers that work can only be done by perfect people who never sin.
- Prayers cannot be prayed in the car, at the laundromat, or in the drive-thru at McDonald's.

LEARNING TO PRAY CAN BE MESSY

I am so thankful God allows us to mess up along the way of learning how to be a Christ-follower. Can you imagine the prayers of the disciples? I am sure they made all kinds of mistakes as they learned how to pray and talk to God. What is amazing is that they were talking to God constantly, just as they had their entire lives, and for all of those precious years they were with Him, they just didn't fully realize it yet. They were talking about everything from fishing to the smell of Simon's feet. (Now while I can't prove that they actually discussed Simon's feet, I believe these guys were opening up about a lot of things as they were working to follow Him and become fishers of men.) While they were walking and talking with Jesus, they were walking and talking with God. They were learning how to talk to Him and how to listen to Him. They were learning how to understand what He was teaching and to obey Him.

Today you may feel like you are still learning how to pray, and your prayers just don't measure up to the prayers of Brother-So-and-So or Elder-Right-and-Ready, but you need to know this: God does not accept your prayers based on your position in life or on how eloquent they sound. He accepts them based upon the finished work of His Son and your sincere faith in Him.

> **God does not accept your prayers based on your position in life or on how eloquent they sound. He accepts them based upon the finished work of His Son and your sincere faith in Him.**

Have you ever wondered if your prayers were of value to God? Then you are not alone. I am sure the disciples did as well, but without them even knowing it they were with Christ, enrolled in the school of prayer. Andrew Murray's classic book *With Christ in The School of Prayer*,[3] is full of powerful reflections about the incredible relationship He developed with His followers as He taught them how to pray, and modeled it for them as well. It is something that Jesus never taught His disciples how to stand up in a temple or on a hillside and preach. In fact, He seemed to challenge them, especially when they faced persecution, to trust the Holy Spirit to give them the words they needed. That does not mean that God is opposed to learning and preparation for those who are called to teach or preach, it simply points to this critical priority: Jesus never taught any of them how to preach, but He did teach them how to pray.

PRAYER BEGINS WITH A QUESTION

One of my favorite encounters in the Bible (and I happen to think it's one of Jesus' favorites as well) is when one of His disciples asked Him to teach them how to pray. Later in this book we will go much deeper into the famous prayer, but let me share it here for the sake of an illustration.

> Now it came to pass, as He was praying in a certain place, when He ceased, that one of His disciples said to Him, "Lord, teach us to pray, as John also taught his disciples."
>
> So He said to them, "When you pray, say:
>
> "Our Father in heaven,
> Hallowed be Your name.
> Your kingdom come.
> Your will be done
> On earth as it is in heaven.
> Give us day by day our daily bread.
> And forgive us our sins,
> For we also forgive everyone who is indebted to us.
> And do not lead us into temptation,
> But deliver us from the evil one." Luke 11:1-4

In my mind, up until this point these disciples were just like me. They had been praying mostly about monsters and girlfriends, the things that mattered most to their own life. But then as they walked and talked with Jesus, they saw something happening. They saw very key moments just before or after His times of teaching and ministry that He withdrew to pray.

They noticed He would often withdraw himself from everyone else to go into the wilderness by Himself to pray. Now, while the Bible does not tell us how often this happened, it does seem like it happened quite often. It kind of reminds me of a scene I can remember in one of the Superman movies where someone starts to notice that Clark Kent is never around when Superman shows up. I can imagine the disciples are noticing over time that powerful connection between the time that Jesus went away to pray in secret and what happens in plain sight. I can almost see someone say, "Okay, He goes away to pray and then He shows up and says things we have never heard before. He goes on a prayer walk, and now, we are seeing miracles that only God can do. What is He doing when He goes to pray?" At this point, they had seen and heard enough that they knew this prayer life that they didn't understand was somehow linked to incredible results they were seeing in the open.

Like me, these disciples had started with monsters and girlfriends, but now they were ready to learn a new way of praying. Without them fully grasping what they were asking for, they were ready to go from praying for what they could see, to praying for what they could not see. They were asking for an open door, without knowing what was behind it. They were about to be taught how to pray kingdom prayers, instead of just earthly prayers. I can only imagine how that request must have thrilled Jesus. It would be like a son finally asking a father to show him how he made a car run better, or a daughter asking a mother how she made her homemade mashed potatoes and famous fried chicken. Everything changed when they asked Christ to teach them how to pray. You have not, because you ask not, and what the disciples had asked Jesus for was the key to learning how to not only pray for the needs, but for His kingdom to come to earth as it is in Heaven. Christ was about to teach them how to Pray for Reign.

YOUR PRAYERS MATTER

If you have ever felt like your prayers seem meaningless and without power, you're not alone. There have been many who felt the same way, including many of the original disciples. What you need to know and remember is that every great prayer warrior started at the same place everyone else did. They didn't really know how to pray in the beginning, they just had a need or desire and God used that to draw them into the most amazing world they could ever imagine.

Rees Howells didn't start off his journey of being a prayer giant by praying for the defeat of Hitler at one of the most crucial times in modern-day history. Most likely, he started his prayer journey by asking God to help him make more money or get a better job. Like me, he may have begun with praying for monsters and girlfriends, but that was only the beginning and a bridge to learning a whole new way of praying—one that possibly changed the outcome of WWII. If he was like me, he went from praying the prayers that originated out of his own pain and desires to praying the prayers that originated out of Heaven.

There are five kinds of people who will read this book. Where do you fit?

The Prayer Apprentice. This is where everyone begins: at the apprentice level. It's what I referred to earlier as the "monsters and girlfriends" stage, where prayer begins but does not end. The person who is beginning in this category is primarily praying for the things they personally need. It's still an important place to learn and experience prayer as you grow in your walk with Jesus.

In this stage, you may find yourself praying for your job or you may be praying for relief from the pressures of bills or debt. Maybe you are praying for personal breakthrough in your marriage or family. All of these things matter, and even as you grow in your prayer life, you will always pray over these things, even as the depth of your prayers expand.

If you are currently in this stage, please know that the things you are praying about matter to God greatly. They matter because you matter to Him. You are His child and He loves you and cares for you very much. He loves to hear your petitions because He loves to hear from your heart, but He also wants to share some of the things that are on His heart.

The Prayer Warrior. God's desire is to meet you in your apprenticeship and help you to grow into a mature son or daughter, what I will call the prayer warrior. If you can imagine a father who not only desires for his child to work in the family business but eventually help him to run it, then you are beginning to grasp what Praying for Reign is all about. It starts with being an apprentice, one who is primarily focused on the needs of self, to becoming a mature heir focused on the needs of the family business, the kingdom of God.

Slowly, Father God will call the apprentice out to deeper and deeper water. The first step into deeper water might be to pray for the next election; to stand in the gap regarding a hot-button issue or a candidate in the running. That next step might be to pray for the little old lady who lives just down the street whom He wants to touch, all because He needs you to partner with Him in prayer to accomplish what He desires. I have heard it said more than once that while God does not need our permission, He does seek and require our agreement in prayer. God wants to hear your prayers, even for monsters and girlfriends, because He knows that those are the beginnings of calling us into becoming an heir. From those first prayers, every invitation to come deeper in prayer is really an invitation to come deeper into the family business of the King. It's called the kingdom of God and prayer in the kingdom of God is called Praying for Reign.

> I have heard it said more than once that while God does not need our permission, He does seek and require our agreement in prayer.

The Retired Prayer Warrior. This person Prayed for Reign in the past, even if it was for a short season in their life, but now they feel like they are too old to make a difference. They may feel it's time for younger leaders with greater influence to lead the charge. Nothing could be farther from the truth! While it's true that we all slow down in our activity as we get older, that should never be the case for our intercession. Later in this book you will read how two elderly sisters, one blind the other disabled, were both pivotal in interceding for a powerful revival. Dear saint of God, it's not time to retire from prayer; it's time for you to understand that you do not have to be young and strong to be effective in prayer. The one thing I would like to encourage every retired person to understand is that not only can they still be a powerful prayer warrior for the kingdom, they may actually have more time to do it. Even if God uses you to focus your prayers upon your children and grandchildren, you have a purpose and a destiny and you can still Pray for Reign.

The Wounded Prayer Warrior. This person has been wounded in battle, maybe through great disappointment or hurt. The enemy is hoping that you put your weapon down for good, and not just for a short time to heal. When you are wounded, it is so important to return to base and heal, but it is equally important that you continue to pray. You may have prayed your heart out for something to happen only to have it not occur as you desired. Those big unanswered prayers can seem devastating, but even if you were strongly disappointed, it does not mean you are not called to pray. Sometimes the things we pray for—yes, even those things we strongly believe God called us to agree with Him on—don't come to pass as we hope. Many times disappointment or hope deferred can cause a warrior to lose their confidence and strength. This happened to King David when he and his men returned to their camp at Ziklag:

> Now it happened, when David and his men came to Ziklag, on the third day, that the Amalekites had invaded the South and Ziklag, attacked Ziklag and burned it with fire, and had taken captive the women and those who were there, from small to great; they did

not kill anyone, but carried them away and went their way. 1 Samuel 30:1-2

David was devastated. It appeared he had lost everything he'd fought and hoped for. You may have felt this way after you prayed for someone to be healed and they were not. You may have prayed for your marriage, holding to the promise that God would save it, but in the end you still found yourself standing in a broken home filled with heartache and disappointment. The enemy is betting that we'll take more than a break to heal and rise to fight again.

One of the things I love most from the story of the rescued soldiers at Dunkirk is what they did next. You would have thought such a defeat at the hands of the enemy would have discouraged them from ever engaging in battle again. While many of them did return safely to England, most of them also went back to become part of the allied force that eventually toppled Germany. David felt defeated, I am sure, but the Bible declares that he didn't dwell there. Instead, he encouraged himself and reengaged the enemy:

> Now David was greatly distressed, for the people spoke of stoning him, because the soul of all the people was grieved, every man for his sons and his daughters. But David strengthened himself in the LORD his God.

> Then David said to Abiathar the priest, Ahimelech's son, "Please bring the ephod here to me." And Abiathar brought the ephod to David. So David inquired of the LORD, saying, "Shall I pursue this troop? Shall I overtake them?"

> And He answered him, "Pursue, for you shall surely overtake them and without fail recover all." 1 Samuel 30:6-8

While it may not be possible to put your broken marriage back together again or raise that lost friend whom you prayed for back from the dead, it is possible to be used again by God in prayer. It is possible to see God use your prayers to shape and save a person or even a nation. The enemy hopes you will retreat and no longer engage in prayer like an heir. However, God wants you to come to Him so that you can once again encourage yourself in Him. He wants you to heal, but then He wants you to pick up that flag again like the character

> **Great loss can steal our confidence in prayer, but a great God can restore it once again.**

Benjamin Martin did in the climactic battle scene at the end of the movie *The Patriot*. Great loss can steal our confidence in prayer, but a great God can restore it once again.

The Disengaged Prayer Warrior. The last Prayer Warrior listed here may be the saddest, but there is still great hope for them. One of the enemy's greatest weapons is the weapon of condemnation. He not only loves to trip God's people up, but once they have fallen, he encourages them to stay down. Once someone has fallen or backslidden, the enemy is going to tell them to stay where they are at, that they are no longer qualified to be used by God. I believe the next great move of God is going to be triggered by the prayers of the prodigals who have finally come home. Even now as I write this, I hear the Lord saying, "Can these bones live again? Can they become a great and mighty army?" I say, "Just watch and see what God is about to do with those returning sons and daughters."

When the prodigal son returned, he did not have to live with the pigs for five years before he could return to the father's house and ultimately the father's business. No, a ring was placed on his finger the day he returned. You may be reading this and thinking you have to get back in line before God will use you in prayer again. I am here to tell you that you do not have to go to the back of the line and start over. True, you may need healing or counseling, that's just using wisdom, but for prayer, you only need to do a U-turn and reengage again. It's not only time to come home, it's also time to join the family business again. It's time to Pray for Reign.

No matter where you may be in your prayer journey, God wants to take you deeper and farther than you have ever been before. He not only wants to teach us how to pray, but also to teach us why prayer is so important. More than ever we need the prayer army to arise and for every follower of Christ to understand that this battle is not just for the seasoned prayer warriors, it's for all of us.

Chapter Three

START AT GO!

To Understand Praying for Reign,
You Must Start at the Beginning

I have always loved playing the board game Monopoly. You can ask my kids; I am always trying to talk them into playing with me on holidays or long family vacations. I don't know why, but it's hard to get them to play with me. Maybe it's because I don't negotiate a lot, or maybe it's because I always want the little dog piece, or maybe it's just because I win a lot. Well, thank goodness for my six grandchildren who are just getting old enough to beat—ahem, I mean *play with*. It's a classic game that I love so much, my family even bought me a deluxe edition, which comes encased in a wooden frame with drawers for the money. It takes two people to set it up, and it takes up the whole dining room table, but it's amazing.

PRAYING FOR REIGN STARTS IN GENESIS

To play the game of Monopoly, you have to start at "go." Likewise, if you are going to understand how wonderful prayer really is, you need to start at "go." The beginning of prayer coincides with the origin of our story, located in the Book of Genesis. It's a deep and wonderful mystery what God was thinking when He formed man and put him in the garden. There are some things we can read and learn from.

GOD PUT MAN IN CHARGE

> Then God said, "Let Us make man in Our image, according to Our likeness; let them have dominion over the fish of the sea, over the birds of the air, and over the cattle, over all the earth and over every creeping thing that creeps on the earth." So God created man in His own image; in the image of God He created him; male and female He created them. Then God blessed them, and God said to them, "Be fruitful and multiply; fill the earth and subdue it; have dominion over the fish of the sea, over the birds of the air, and over every living thing that moves on the earth." Genesis 1:26-28

In the beginning, when God created man and woman and put them in the garden, He put them in charge; He gave them dominion. In other words, He gave them the keys. This was further confirmed as He created all of the animals and then brought them to Adam to name.

> And the LORD God said, "It is not good that man should be alone; I will make him a helper comparable to him." Out of the ground the Lord God formed every beast of the field and every bird of the air, and brought them to Adam to see what he would call them. And whatever Adam called each living creature, that was its name. So Adam gave names to all cattle, to the birds of the air, and to every beast of the field. But for Adam there was not found a helper comparable to him. Genesis 2:18-20

Naming something demonstrates that the person giving the name has the authority to do so. The fact that God called Adam to name His creations solidifies that Adam was more than just another one of God's creations; he was also crafted to be a participant in the creation process alongside God. The naming of the animals actually illustrates the earliest picture of prayer: a partnership between God and man, one where they worked together for the purposes of God. Why would God want to form a partnership with His creation? One in which the man had the opportunity to fail or succeed?

> The naming of the animals actually illustrates the earliest picture of prayer: a partnership between God and man, one where they worked together for the purposes of God.

GOD WANTED A FAMILY

You may be asking yourself, "What was God thinking? Why would God risk His creation and everything He wanted on a man?" I believe God didn't just desire to create a living being who was good at gardening and serving Him; God desired something more. I believe God yearned to create someone who was like Him, made in His image and likeness. God wanted to create a family.

Think about it; if God simply wanted to keep creating beings to worship Him, He could have stuck to creating more angels. But even with God's creation of the angels, we see that our Heavenly Father didn't just want a large stash of lifeless statues to fill the halls of Heaven; He wanted a kingdom of children and angelic beings who loved Him, worshipped Him, and really wanted to be with Him.

Born of that same desire, we see that God even gave Lucifer the power to choose. Why did He give Adam and Eve the power to choose whether they would obey when it came to eating from the Tree of the Knowledge of Good and Evil? God gave all of us the power to choose because love cannot be love without a choice. Can you imagine if your spouse had been forced to marry you, if they had not been given a choice? That would not be love. Our Heavenly Father wanted sons and daughters, ones who decided to be one with Him of their own free will.

> **God gave all of us the power to choose because love cannot be love without a choice.**

Understanding the purpose behind creation is so vital if we are ever going to understand why we exist and why God made us. While it's true we were made for His pleasure, it's important to understand what brings God pleasure. The cornerstone of understanding what brings God pleasure can be found in His Word.

PLEASING GOD BEGINS WITH BELIEVING HIM

"But without faith *it is* impossible to please *Him,* for he who comes to God must believe that He is, and *that* He is a rewarder of those who diligently seek Him." Hebrews 11:6. God desires not only for us to believe *in* Him, but more importantly, to *believe Him.* It's almost like God is establishing everything on this truth: that pleasing Him or bringing Him pleasure begins with what we believe. To please God, we must believe that He is who He says He is. This means that we not only believe what He says about Himself, but also about us.

That last one is a hard one for a lot of people. Many find it's easier to believe what God says about Himself than to believe what He says about them. Why does pleasing Him begin with what we believe about Him? Some think pleasing Him has nothing to do with belief, but everything to do with our actions. If you feed the poor and help the homeless, doesn't that please Him? God truly desires for His children to show compassion—it reflects who He is—but He is looking for something more than just good works. The Lord spoke this truth into my spirit one day as I was praying, and it changed how I saw everything and helped me understand Him more:

"I'm not looking for people to do things for me … I am looking for people to do things with me!"

As I meditated on that truth, it became clear that God's not looking for people to just do good things for Him. Yes, like us, it pleases Him to no end when His kids do the right things, the things that He desires, but He is looking for something more. He wants to be more than just our Creator; He also wants to be an active participant in our life. He is a good Father, and He also wants us to be a participant in His ongoing work, to be part of what He is doing. That is what Praying for Reign is all about. Praying for Reign is partnering and agreeing with God through prayer for the fulfillment of His plan—His plan to manifest His kingdom realm on earth as it is in Heaven.

> "I'm not looking for people to do things for me…I am looking for people to do things with me!"

In the beginning, this partnership appeared as God was creating the animals and having Adam to name them. Today, this partnership can manifest as God calling us to prayer-walk through our neighborhood. Think about it; while God is the only one who can bring your neighbors into salvation and new life, He calls on you to be the person who calls on Him to do it. He creates, but we participate with Him in prayer and then in action.

One of the most misunderstood concepts regarding this partnership is this: while God will do amazing things with our participation (specifically in the area of prayer), He will not do so without us playing our part. To mortal man, that just does not make sense. Isn't God sovereign? Why would He desire or need our participation in prayer? Once you can understand this truth—that God in His absolute sovereignty designed a plan that requires our participation—then you can understand what prayer is all about and why we are called to Pray for Reign.

THE SOVEREIGNTY OF GOD

God is absolutely and without question sovereign. What does sovereignty actually mean? The best definition is that God has supreme power. God is absolutely the supreme power of the world and the entire universe. He is the supreme power of it all!

It can also mean autonomy. Autonomy is the state of existing or acting separately from others. God is autonomous in Himself, as He does not need us to exist. He needs no one to exist to be God, but that does not mean that He did not, in His infinite wisdom, design mankind with a part He needed us to play.

GOD TEACHES US TO DRIVE

There are so many metaphors in daily life that mimic this act of God putting the control into our hands. I always picture a father who is teaching his son or daughter to drive. As he teaches, he is in the passenger seat, and at any time he can tell his child to stop or turn right. Eventually, the day comes where the father is there, but he is allowing his child to drive without his interference. Outside of a wrong move or decision that could cause a crash, the father is allowing the son to drive without intruding. He is there to guide if needed, but the father knows he has to allow his child to make some decisions or he will never learn how to really drive. The father knows that one day, his son or daughter will pull out of the driveway on their own, and he will not be able to provide moment-by-moment guidance. He wants his child to learn how to be like him, and the only way to do that is to eventually put him in full control of the car.

The father could stay in control of the car at all times, even driving the child as they progress into adulthood. That may sound strange, but I actually know someone who did that, driving their children into their early twenties. He didn't do it because they only had one car or because his children had issues that would keep them from being safe drivers;

he did it because he was afraid to give them control of the vehicle. In the end, it not only hurt the growth of the children, it also hurt their relationship as a family.

Our Heavenly Father is absolutely supreme, and He is in control of the entire universe, but He has given us the keys to earth. If you have any doubts of this, just look at the journey of man here on the earth. It's clear there have been a lot of crashes and wrecks over the years. It's important to understand that God has given us dominion, but it is not the dominion of an absent father who has left us on our own to make it or lose everything. Nothing could be further from the truth. Our Heavenly Father wants us to drive the car and make the decisions, but He is actively working to draw us toward making the right decisions, the ones that will follow the wonderful plan He has for our lives and future.

GOD GAVE US DOMINION

God gives us dominion with the oversight and influence of a loving Father. Is God involved in the affairs of man? Yes! Every single second of every single day God is working to establish His kingdom in the hearts of every man, woman and child. Unlike some of the fathers of our day, our Heavenly Father is never absent and is always seeking time with us, and creating ways to influence and help us. If I was to use the car analogy again, He has planned out a wonderful trip for us to go on. He has provided a map, the fuel, the lodging, and everything else we need to make the trip. Best of all, even though He allows us to drive and decide where we are going, He never leaves us. He is always there to guide us and help draw us back to the plan He has drawn out.

While the truth that God is sovereign is not debatable, it is also one of the most misunderstood things in the church today. The part that is misconstrued is the idea that because God is sovereign, He does whatever He wants despite our actions or input. Over the years, I have heard Christians make the following statement: "It really does not matter if I pray or not, God is sovereign and He is going to do whatever He wants to do anyway." I actually think the greatest deterrent to prayer is the misunderstanding of the sovereignty of God.

In Paul E. Billheimer's classic book *Destined for the Throne*[4] the author shares his powerful stance on why God has given us dominion on earth and why God created prayer as the main means for us to overcome obstacles and experience victory. According to Bilheimer, in the end, it's God's master plan of creating a bride for His Son. Through the exercise of believing prayer, the church has been given the opportunity to experience warfare and struggle, but more importantly, victory. It is through this dynamic struggle that we are ultimately being trained and prepared to share the throne with Christ as His bride. It makes perfect sense if you really think about it. Prayer is training for reigning.

ARE WE NEEDED TO HELP GOD FINISH HIS PLAN ON EARTH?

A larger question may be: "Are we needed to complete God's plan on earth? Does the Body of Christ have a part to play that God will not force or override?"

Before I answer that question, let me remind you of the incorrect views of sovereignty many Christians hold and how it can deter the work of the church. The problem comes when we think God is going to do whatever He is going to do, no matter what we do. For example, someone fails to pray for their nation because they think, "Well, God is sovereign and He is going to do what He wants whether I pray or not." All one has to do is look in the Bible to understand this is not true. Just look at what the prophet Ezekiel wrote regarding the need for an intercessor to complete God's plan:

> "So I sought for a man among them who would make
> a wall, and stand in the gap before Me on behalf of the
> land, that I should not destroy it; but I found no one."
> Ezekiel 22:30

Now, if we were to use some of the misunderstandings of our day regarding sovereignty, this scripture would have read something like this:

"So I sought for a man among them who would make a wall, and stand in the gap before Me on behalf of the land, that I should not destroy it; but I found no one so I just stepped in and did it myself."

Nothing should awaken our call to pray like this. God has put some matters into our hands, and if we do nothing, God will not override us. To do that would derail His entire plan of creating an overcoming church and a bride for His Son who is prepared to reign with Christ for eternity. The famous John Wesley quote makes more sense than ever when you understand this principle: "God does nothing except in response to believing prayer."

The only time we see a deviation from this principal is when God came to earth to do what only He could do, which was to provide a sacrifice for our sins. But don't miss this point: while God stepped in to do what we couldn't do for ourselves, He had to come as a man to do it. Why? Because God had given man dominion over the earth. For Him to come to influence the earth, He had to actually become incarnate. That is why the incarnation is the most amazing thing ever. It not only showcases God's extreme love for us, but it also showcases His infinite wisdom. God gave dominion of the earth to man, but in the fall, man lost it to Satan. God could not violate His word, or He would not be God. He had to create a plan that did not violate His word but executed an opening for salvation and gave dominion back to His kids once again.

To fully understand the key position we hold in prayer, we must go back to the beginning, to the story God began composing about our lives and His eternal plan for us, His children. This understanding is truly a game-changer and the whole foundation to understanding what Praying for Reign is all about.

It is so exciting when we truly understand how prayer is a component of God's eternal plan for His children, one in which they can truly partner with Him. It is with that understanding that we learn prayer is more about God getting our attention than us getting His. As you read further along in this book, you will see how this statement is so

> **Prayer is more about God getting our attention than us getting His.**

true. God is more than ready to hear the cries from our heart for help, but He also wants us to hear what is on His heart. When we do, we find out He is calling us into the most amazing place in prayer, one in which we participate in His plan of not only building a family but also a kingdom.

When you look at the wonderful story of how God intended to create a family—one that would truly live and reign with Him throughout eternity—you see a beautiful picture of the ongoing plan of redemption; a plan of redemption not just for the way things were but more for the way things were really supposed to be. Think of this plan in the simple terms of a series of scenes.

- Scene One: God created man in His likeness and image. He put man in charge, giving him the keys.
- Scene Two: Man fell short of God's glory by following Satan's deception, so man gave up those keys to Satan and put Satan and his kingdom in charge.
- Scene Three: In God's mercy and eternal plan, He sent His only Son in the form of a man to pay the ultimate price for our sins. Christ not only opened the door for our salvation, He also took back the keys from Satan.
- Scene Four: When Christ instituted His church, He gave back to Peter and the church the keys that Adam and Eve once held. God restored things to the way they should be.

Now the church, through the work of Christ, holds those keys once again. Satan and his network of evil principalities and powers do not hold those keys anymore. While the enemy still possesses the same power of deception that was displayed in the Garden of Eden, we now have the power to resist it and overcome it.

It's true that we still live in a fallen world filled with tragedy and difficulty, but we must remember that Satan can never defeat the true church as it walks once again in the delegated power and authority that God has granted it. Does that mean everything turns out like we want it to? Of course not, but it does not mean that we have to be held captive to Satan's lies and deception. The church now holds the keys and the only questions are: Do we believe that? Are we using those keys? And are we Praying for Reign?

Chapter Four

FEARFULLY AND WONDERFULLY MADE

Becoming the Person God Created You to Be Through Praying for Reign

D o you know who you really are in Christ, or do you struggle to fully understand who God has made you to be? If you do, then know that you are not alone. The majority of Christians struggle with self-worth and believing who they really are as a child of God.

Sadly, many Christians view salvation only as a change in their eternal destination and not a change in who they are. It's a wonderful mystery that as we are born again, we receive both an invitation to Heaven when we die and a connection to Heaven here and now on earth. It comes because of God's kingdom coming to fruition inside of us when we go through the transformation from being children of darkness to becoming children of light.

It's a wonderful mystery that as we are born again, we receive both an invitation to Heaven when we die and a connection to Heaven here and now on earth.

MISTAKEN IDENTITY

Many Christians struggle with what we could refer to as "mistaken identity." When I was a state trooper, I dealt with this concept more than a few times. I remember a time when someone was mistakenly identified as a wanted person. Before long, everyone was on the lookout for this person. When he was eventually stopped, we were all shocked to find out he was just an auto mechanic who happened to be wearing the same color jacket that was worn by the actual perpetrator. While those reports were necessary to help us find the real suspect, they are not necessary in the kingdom of God. The enemy loves to identify us as suspects and "lost children" with no future in hope that we will believe it. God, however, wants you to know and believe what He has said about you and prayer.

You see, if you have accepted Christ as your Savior and you call Him Lord, then you are not just getting a wonderful eternal destination called Heaven; you are now a totally different person. You might ask yourself, "If I am really different, then why don't I feel different? Why do I struggle with the same things I struggled with before I became a Christian? I feel good about myself when I go to church, but during the week it's a struggle."

> **Prayer is not only the vehicle through which God translates His desires to you, but it's also where He translates your kingdom identity and purpose.**

What would you say if I told you that prayer is not only the vehicle through which God translates His desires to you, but it's also where He translates your kingdom identity and purpose?

A LESSON FROM WALES

In 2002, I took a trip with my wife and daughter to the country of Wales. We were going there for a week to participate in a crusade being led back then by the late Steve Hill of the Brownsville Revival. This was my first trip overseas, and I cannot tell you how excited I was to be in Wales to join Steve and many others as they held meetings at the birthplace of the Welsh Revival. If you are not a student of revivals, the Welsh Revival was a powerful move of God that occurred from 1904-1905. While the revival did not last for years and years, the effects of it have lasted until this day. It was an amazing, spontaneous, and sovereign move of the Spirit of God in response to believing prayer.

On this trip, we were to join Steve and his team in Swansea, Wales. I was filled with the greatest anticipation as I navigated our rented vehicle across the M-4, traveling from London to Southern Wales. When planning this trip, I thought that with my experience as a state trooper, I would not have any issues driving on the wrong side of the road and driving a car with a manual transmission. Was I wrong about that! The M-4 is like an interstate, so driving that portion was not that bad. Once I entered Wales, however, I had to navigate roads with signs I couldn't read and roundabouts I couldn't get out of. The trip became a nightmare. I had been warned to expect spiritual warfare on this trip because it involved a pivotal series of meetings with the purpose to bring breakthrough to Wales once again. There was no doubt that I was fending off some kind of attack as I drove toward our hotel in Swansea.

The difficulties caused us to run behind, and we missed the first meeting. It had been raining off and on, as it does in Great Britain, and now it was dark. Finally, in desperation, I waved down a taxi and paid him to lead us to our hotel. I think he could tell I was very lost.

Have you ever gone through uncharted waters and felt lost? You start out all excited and full of vision, and then it seems that everything and everyone who was there to cheer you on disappears. I am sure that is what Charles Lindbergh felt as he was crossing the Atlantic Ocean on his way to Paris, France. While following God can lead you into some lonely places that will test your own belief—not to mention your family's—it's what waits on the other side that makes it so worth it. For me, I was getting ready to have the most powerful spiritual experience in my life, and this experience would eventually teach me how prayer is the key to discovering who we really are in Christ.

After we arrived to the hotel, I had my wife Tracee and daughter Ashlee go ahead to our hotel room while I parked and moved the luggage inside. I was so relieved to finally be at the hotel, and now I was just trying to get everything into the room so I could crash in the bed. It was well after midnight as our four-hour journey had turned into a seven-hour nightmare. When I finally got to the room, my wife and daughter were already in bed, and my wife informed me that she had kindly drawn a hot bath for

> **Prayer is the key to discovering who we really are in Christ.**

me. I don't know if she knew that I needed it after the whole event of getting there, or if it was her kind way of telling me I didn't smell good. Either way, I was eager to have a hot bath before I jumped into bed for the night.

There are times when God shows up in your life and you feel like you have done nothing to have earned it. Hundreds of times we pray and worship, and although much is happening, we might not feel anything. Then there are times God just shows up when you least expect Him, and it's overwhelming. This was one of those times.

As I slipped into the hot bath and allowed the water to wash away my day, the atmosphere began to change dramatically. It was not like any other experience I have ever had with the Lord. I have wept. I have had goose bumps. I have been overwhelmed with a sense of awe during worship and other deep experiences where God had touched me. This encounter was not like any of those experiences.

In this experience, a peace that passes all understanding was all over me; in fact, it was inside of me. I also felt a deep confidence that I can only describe as totally complete. In short, it was as if I didn't need anything to be completely sure of who I was in Christ. This was not self-confidence; this was God's assurance—assurance of who I really was. At the same time that I was experiencing this unreal and complete confidence, there was also an incredible sense of humility. It was like I did not need to be first or the greatest or anything. The only thing I wanted to do was serve God and others because I was complete. To top it off, there was a soft but powerful joy that was running through me. I'm sure I had a smile upon my face.

This experience continued for what seemed like hours. It was like I had become a totally different person, but it was still me—the real me. As I continued to bask in this incredible place, God began to speak to me.

At first I thought they were my thoughts, but I later realized they were His thoughts in me. The first thought was that there would never be any doubt, any depression, any need to prove anything anymore. It was the description of what I was experiencing; that in the reality of peace, purpose, strength and humility, there would never be the presence of those things.

I thought to myself, "Is this what Heaven is like?" As that thought passed, God showed me a picture. The picture was of Christians in the great Roman circus preparing to die for their belief in Christ. As I looked at the picture, it was like I could see their faces, and they were at total and complete peace, actually smiling with a joy that most people never experience, at least in this world. I knew at that moment that I was experiencing a similar peace. This was the most amazing thing I had ever experienced; I have no idea what I did to gain it or why it even happened, but it was real. While the experience eventually ended, I have never forgotten it, and it led me to understand the connection between prayer and learning who we really are in Christ.

> **This was not self-confidence; this was God's assurance—assurance of who I really was.**

I spent a lot time after that trip analyzing that experience to try to understand what it was, and more importantly, how I could return to it. I remember a conversation I had with God a few months later where I asked, "Lord, do you know what that felt like to me?" I prefaced my next statement with: "Lord, I know this is not good theology, but it's the only word-picture I can use to describe how I felt. In that moment, it felt like I was a child of yours who had come to earth from Heaven at your direction to live a life in this world." Of course, I made no comparisons to the Son of God (I am created and He is not), but it was like I was really one of His children.

It was several years later when the Lord actually explained to me what that encounter was all about. Out of the blue, He asked me: "Don, do you want to know what you experienced in that bathtub in Wales?" My obvious response was, "Absolutely!" He told me, "Most people live in this realm—Earth—and try to visit that realm, Heaven. But I allowed you to experience the opposite: what it is like to live in that realm—Heaven—but visit this realm."

> **"Most people live in this realm—Earth—and try to visit that realm, Heaven. But I allowed you to experience the opposite: what it is like to live in that realm—Heaven—but visit this realm."**

Think about it; when you and I have our identity, self-worth, heritage, and ancestry based in Heaven and not on earth, it changes how we view our lives, and it changes how we view ourselves. Through our relationship with Jesus Christ, we are born again, which means we are born from above. When this becomes reality for us, our whole viewpoint of who we are will change. We are different, and there is nothing else we need to do to establish that. It's just as true as if we were born in a palace. The Bible says in 1 Peter 2:9, "But you *are* a chosen generation, a royal priesthood, a holy nation, His own special people, that you may proclaim the praises of Him who called you out of darkness into His marvelous light."

PRAYER CHANGES OUR IDENTITY

The Holy Spirit explained to me that I had experienced this so I could learn how to live this way on earth and teach others about this reality. I felt as if God had miraculously shown me a hidden treasure city, one that changed me just by seeing it, but now He was encouraging me to find the way back to it, the way back to living in His power on earth.

Even though I knew there was no ritual needed to get back to that spot, my mind was filled with thoughts of "How?" It finally became clear how we can experience that deep knowing on a daily basis, the one that comes from God, our source. The way to have our identity centered in Him, knowing who we truly are in Christ, is the way of prayer. While the journey to the deeper life in God that we all hunger for involves both His Word and active obedience, it cannot happen without having a real and vibrant prayer life. Prayer is the vehicle that moves us from just existence to knowing and experiencing who we really are in Christ.

Our identity changes when we pray because prayer unites us with God. It is through prayer that we become like Him as His kingdom is moved from Heaven to earth, not just in us but ultimately through us. In prayer, it can sometimes seem as if we are being moved to Heaven as well, in this wonderfully mysterious place where Heaven meets earth. A praying saint stands on earth, but they are strangely seated in heavenly places while they stand in prayer.

> **Prayer is the vehicle that moves us from just existence to knowing and experiencing who we really are in Christ.**

While prayer always seems focused on the outcome of what we are praying for, something equally (or more) important occurs when we pray. You see, it is through the exercise of prayer that God enables us to really see who we truly are, the person He always intended us to be. For this reason, prayer is not just our partnering with God to establish His kingdom; it's also partnering with

> **Our identity changes when we pray because prayer unites us with God.**

Him in establishing our true identity. It's almost like God gave us this gift of prayer so that we could become who we were always meant to be.

One day when I was in prayer, the Lord spoke into my heart, "When I can become in you who you were always meant to be, you will then begin to look a lot more like Me."

Have you ever heard the saying "You become like the people you hang out with?" I have even seen pictures online or in magazine ads where a man with long blond hair is sitting beside a dog with long blond hair, implying that they have been together long enough that they now look like each other. Prayer is the connection point not just for getting our requests answered; it's also where His kingdom gets into us. We change and become more like Jesus as we spend more time with Him.

> **"When I can become in you who you were always meant to be, you will then begin to look a lot more like Me."**

The reason this is so important is because many in the church are experiencing a severe identity crisis. They don't know who they really are in Christ. They suffer from mistaken identity, a condition that allows them to mistake themselves for someone other than who God made them to be.

> **Many in the church are experiencing a severe identity crisis. They don't know who they really are in Christ. They suffer from mistaken identity, a condition that allows them to mistake themselves for someone other than who God made them to be.**

In the Garden of Eden, it's clear that Eve must have simply forgotten, or she did not realize, that she was already like God when the serpent said in Genesis 3:1-4:

> Now the serpent was more cunning than any beast of the field which the Lord God had made. And he said to the woman, "Has God indeed said, 'You shall not eat of

every tree of the garden'?" And the woman said to the serpent, "We may eat the fruit of the trees of the garden; but of the fruit of the tree which is in the midst of the garden, God has said, "You shall not eat it, nor shall you touch it, lest you die."

Then the serpent said to the woman, "You will not surely die. For God knows that in the day you eat of it your eyes will be opened, and you will be like God, knowing good and evil."

PRAYER IS ALL ABOUT A PARTNERSHIP

While there is no replacement for the Word of God, the belief in our new identity comes from spending time with God. It comes through prayer.

When you are praying, you are not only partnering with the eternal God, He is also partnering with you. When He finds someone on earth who is called by His name, who is willing to stand in the gap, then He has found a representative on earth. It is through the powerful partnership of prayer that we not only change things on earth, bringing the kingdom of God before man, but we also bring change with ourselves. We discover who we really are in Christ.

Here are some things we discover in the partnership of prayer with God.

1. We become eternally conscious. We see beyond the day and even our own lifetime.
2. With our souls filled with God's Spirit, the heart of the Father flows into us and through us.
3. We are seated with Christ in heavenly places.
4. We assume our rightful position in Christ.

5. We distance ourselves from condemnation and the failures of the past.
6. Faith rises up with us.
7. We become like Him. Prayer opens up that transfer of identity.
8. We are now able to shift our heart to His purposes and not just our own.

PRAYER CHANGES OUR APPEARANCE

It has been said over the years that the countenance of many great prayer warriors would actually change when they prayed. This goes back through many stories and accounts throughout church history. There are so many stories of martyrs who experienced a transformation while they were praying before their lives were taken. Their faces reflected a reality of a world beyond this world. Have you ever felt that your face could be a reflection of your spirit? That God could so connect you to His kingdom that the reality of your new identity in Christ comes through your face?

There is no greater picture of this in Scripture than that of our Lord Jesus. This moment was captured for us through the writers of three gospels and Peter. Luke wrote: "As He prayed, the appearance of His face was altered, and His robe became white and glistening" (Luke 9:29).

I love how Peter later described it in 2 Peter 1:16-18 of The Passion Translation:

> We were not retelling some masterfully crafted legend when we informed you of the power and appearing of our Lord Jesus Christ, for we saw his magnificence and splendor unveiled before our very eyes. Yes, Father God lavished upon him radiant glory and honor when his distinct voice spoke out of the realm of majestic glory, endorsing him with these words: This is my cherished Son, marked by my love. All my delight is found in him!

And we ourselves heard that voice resound from the heavens while we were with him on the holy mountain.

While none of us will carry the same glory that the Son of God carried as He prayed, something powerful happens in us and through us as we pray and discover who we really are in Christ. The psalmist in Psalm 34:5 describes it this way: "Gaze upon him, join your life with his, and joy will come. Your faces will glisten with glory. You'll never wear that shame-face again," (Psalm 34:5, TPT).

I love what is said of Brother Lawrence in his classic work *The Practice of the Presence of God*.[2] He often stated that it is God who paints Himself in the depths of our souls. We must merely open our hearts to receive Him and His loving presence.

INTIMACY IS THE GOAL

It is in prayer that we gain intimacy with our Heavenly Father. Being intimate with Him changes our perspective and allows us not only to know Him but also to know who we really are in Him. It's something that while we are praying for the needs of others, toiling in intercession, God is also changing our identity. This is why no one can have a secure and healthy identity in Christ without having an intimate relationship with Him, and that comes primarily through prayer.

> "It is God who paints Himself in the depths of our soul. We must merely open our hearts to receive Him and His loving presence."
> **Brother Lawrence**

Think of how different you feel after you have gone on a vacation or a spiritual retreat. In that time away from the day-to-day, you have allowed yourself the chance to recharge and renew vision. Whether you are aware of it or not, you are recharging and realigning

> Prayer is where you both find yourself and are found by the purposes of God.

yourself every time you return to the place of prayer. Prayer is where you both find yourself and are found by the purposes of God. In prayer, the gifts that are put within you come alive and find their purpose.

Understanding the purpose of prayer, how it enables us to partner with God in the expansion of His kingdom, and also how it helps us to uncover who He created us to be is an amazing experience. As we move forward in this journey of discovering how to Pray for Reign, you will learn why these foundations are so important. They are the bedrock of growth into a great man or woman of prayer.

SECTION TWO

THE GATES OF HELL WILL NOT PREVAIL

How Nothing Is Safe From the Power of Prayer

Chapter Five

TWO WEAK SISTERS

Praying for Reign in Your Church

The power of prayer is unstoppable. There is nothing that is exempt from its effects, especially when it comes to the church. The gates of hell can do nothing to hold back the power of God and His kingdom when His children come into agreement with Him in prayer. As Jesus said to Peter in Matthew 16:18: "And I also say to you that you are Peter, and on this rock I will build My church, and the gates of Hades shall not prevail against it."

> The gates of hell can do nothing to hold back the power of God and His kingdom when His children come into agreement with Him in prayer.

Through centuries of church history, God always had at least one insider who was often hidden from the people's view, but not from His. It was through these unsung heroes of prayer that much has been done to advance the kingdom of God through the church. History truly does belong to the intercessors and those who have committed to prayer, especially praying for the church.

HISTORY CAN BE ONE OF THE GREATEST TEACHERS

If you have never done this before, I would encourage you to go back and read the accounts from the First and Second Great Awakening in America. These awakenings were more than just spiritual markers in America's history; they are like rumble strips that turned our young nation back towards God and steered it away from sure disaster. My great-great-grandfather, Rev. Samuel Newman, came out of the First Great Awakening. The influence of that move of God was so strong that it propelled him to establish one of the first Baptist congregations in South Carolina in 1771. These early Baptist pioneers were known as "New Light" or "Separatist Baptists" and they walked in a power from on-high, much like the early disciples did.

When you read about those who were part of those powerful times of revival, you will learn how God has always used prayer to stir and awaken His church. Deep within those treasured stories of past awakenings are the records of the intercessors who prayed them in. These passionate saints partnered with God in prayer and called for His kingdom in Heaven to invade earth, beginning within His church. Add to these accounts of those early awakenings the stories of other great revivals like the Welsh Revival, and you will begin to see a pattern. All of them have these three things in common:

- The church had become cold and powerless, slowly losing its ability to influence and affect the community.
- Someone picked up the burden for this condition and prayed until there was an answer or a breakthrough.
- God showed up and everything changed.

When you look at the word "Intercession" and begin to discover some of the root words it relates to, you begin to get a picture of someone acting as a "go-between."[5] Using the previous illustration, the intercessor is acting as that "go-between" between a dying church and a powerful, prayer-answering God. Another picture we get from the root of this word is an intersection, where two roads cross or meet. What a powerful illustration this picture paints, one where the intercessor prays until the road that the church is traveling down intersects with the road God is traveling on. Revival and spiritual resurrection always occur where these two roads meet.

> **The intercessor prays until the road that the church is traveling down intersects with the road God is traveling on. Revival and spiritual resurrection always occur where these two roads meet.**

GOD USES PEOPLE JUST LIKE YOU

Did you know that many of those early people who prayed those revivals into being were just like you? These early "prayer troopers," who gave themselves to prayer for the church, were not often trained ministers or clergy, but housewives and laborers who worked regular jobs and had everyday cares. God loves using these unlikely and often unknown people to pray down Heaven to earth. God has been known to use fishermen, tax collectors, and even one time a coal miner to foster a move of His kingdom on earth.

Throughout the years, God has used the very salt of this earth to pray in many of the heaven-sent revivals we read about in church history. Who knows, you might be the next one to join this group! A group made of men and women who, from a private but powerful place of hidden prayer, have moved the unseen into the seen. Through the years of church history, their stories teach us that God only needs one person who is willing to connect with Him to pave a

> **God has been known to use fishermen, tax collectors, and even one time a coal miner to foster a move of His kingdom on earth.**

prayer-intersection between Heaven and earth. One person plus God is always a majority.

THE CHURCH NEEDS AN AWAKENING

Maybe you look at your church and the surrounding community and find yourself discouraged. Discouraged by the condition of both the world and today's church, you may think, "I know God can move, but things have never been worse than now." Or perhaps you think, "I've prayed before, but nothing ever really happened. Why should I pray for revival again?"

When the Lord told me to write this book, He was clear to me that it was a mandate from Him; a mandate to encourage His church to keep praying and for those who had laid down their shields and swords to pick them up once again. The enemy knows that he cannot defeat the church, but he also knows that he doesn't *have* to when the church has been shackled with discouragement and locked up by hope deferred. When that occurs, the church ends up being defeated on its own, and drops not only its spiritual weapons, but much worse its faith.

> The enemy knows that he cannot defeat the church, but he also knows that he doesn't *have* to when the church has been shackled with discouragement and locked up by hope deferred.

If you have ever felt that your prayers for revival and the church just go unanswered, I have good news to share. First, you need to know you are not the only one who has felt this way. I experienced my own spiritual letdown right after the 2020 presidential election. My intention in sharing this is not to create a discussion about politics, but to honestly say I was discouraged by the results of my and other's prayers. It would have been easy for me to have begun to doubt prayer, ultimately withdrawing from the battlefield. It took time but God eventually showed me that my prayers and the prayers of many others were not in vain. It was in this season that God said to me,

"Prayer is not magic; it's warfare. Warfare that can be won if we develop a campaign mentality, not just a battle one."

Everyone experiences what they consider to be unanswered prayers at some point or another. Even Christ Jesus experienced this when He prayed to His Father in Matthew 26:39: "O My Father, if it is possible, let this cup pass from Me; nevertheless, not as I will, but as You *will*." Even though Jesus saw His first request go unanswered, that did not stop Him from continuing to pray. If you have prayed for revival before and felt that your request went

> "Prayer is not magic; it's warfare. Warfare that can be won if we develop a campaign mentality, not just a battle one."

unanswered, you need to know that you're not alone. Others have experienced it as well. More importantly, though, you need to realize that you are not finished.

God wants us to Pray for Reign in His church, and that begins with your very own church and church community. The pastor or minister who has someone that will stand behind them and their work in prayer is not only blessed, they are very fortunate. Even though the work of intercessors often goes without any recognition, it is recognized in Heaven. God wants you to pray for the church, for it's through His church that God births and sustains an awakening.

REVIVAL BEGINS IN THE CHURCH

It seems clear that God's process is to impact His church first, and then through the church, impact the community it exists in. I love the stories from the First Great Awakening in America; how God used prayer and a few key leaders to awaken a cold and lifeless church. There is no doubt that if God did it then, He can do it once again in our lifetime. The church today needs the same fire that fell in Enfield, Connecticut on July 8, 1741, when Jonathan Edwards preached his powerful sermon "Sinners in the Hands of an Angry God." I'll bet that someone prior to that famous meeting had been praying and the fruit of those prayers, as demonstrated through its amazing results, were far and long lasting. They ultimately reached my great-great-grandfather and millions of many others.

My prayer is that someone who is reading this book will feel the call to pray for their church, that God would find in them an instrument He can work in and through to bring forth in that church such a move, such an awakening, that the whole community is eventually changed. You may be reading this and find yourself doubting that one person's prayers could really have that type of impact. I assure you, God can use one man or one woman who is willing to pray until the breakthrough comes to ignite a fire that will eventually engulf a whole community. God is looking for lightning rods of prayer, ones who will dig in and stand with Him in faith and agreement until an awakening breaks out within the church and community.

> **God is looking for lightning rods of prayer, ones who will dig in and stand with Him in faith and agreement until an awakening breaks out within the church and community.**

THE HEBRIDES REVIVAL

In what is one of my favorite stories of revival, God found two—not just one—lightning rods of prayer He could work through in a small group of islands off the west coast of Scotland called the Hebrides. This powerful move of God, referred to as the Hebrides Revival,[6] had its beginning in a small parish church in the village of Barvas, but its origin is tied to two sisters; two sisters who most people would have never chosen as the fire-starters for a move of God.

PEGGY AND CHRISTINE SMITH

Peggy and Christine Smith lived in a small cottage in the village of Barvas, located on the Isle of Lewis within the Hebrides Islands. Prior to the Hebrides Revival, there was great concern within the community for the church. If you were to ask someone from that time for their opinion of the local church, they would have told you that it was not just cold, but headed toward a certain death. Peggy and Christine were at the epicenter of this as they had watched their own parish and the church of their father slowly slip away into a spiritual coma. The gravest concern for these two sisters was the fact that the youth had virtually turned away from the church and wanted nothing to do with it. If you want to know what one of the first signs of a dying church is, its most often seen in a decline in attendance of the young people.

The condition of the church and community burdened Peggy and Christine so greatly that they committed to making prayer a priority. They dedicated themselves to praying for their church and community, and God answered their prayers in a powerful way. Now, unless you are familiar with their story, you might be picturing two ladies who ran the prayer meetings at church or had some position of influence. You can probably name someone like that in your own church. But God does not always choose who *we* would choose to light the fires of a modern-day Pentecost. Many times, God will choose the least likely, basing His choice on the prerequisites of hunger and faith—not position or stature.

God chose Peggy and Christine Smith to be a catalyst in prayer for revival despite their age and their physical condition. Both were over eighty years old, with Peggy being blind and Christine's body so wrecked by arthritis that she was unable to stand up. They were in such bad shape that they were actually unable to attend worship at the church. They may have been unable to leave their cottage, but that did not stop them from entering Heaven in prayer. These two unlikely prayer warriors turned their cottage into a powerful prayer sanctuary, one that God used to shake an entire region of Scotland. These sisters would not necessarily be the first people you would have chosen to help lead a whole community into revival, but as God often does, He uses the weak things of the world to confound the wise.

As these dear sisters bombarded Heaven in prayer, a verse from Isaiah gripped them: "For I will pour water on him who is thirsty, And floods on the dry ground" (Isaiah 44:3). As their mission to pray down Heaven increased, Peggy and Christine made a decision to dedicate two to three days a week specifically for prayer. They would get down on their knees and pray sometimes from ten o'clock at night until three or four in the morning.

One night, after several weeks of praying, one of the sisters had a vision. In this vision, she saw her church filled with young people, like it used to be many years earlier. She also saw a man preaching in the pulpit whom she did not know, but later she would learn that man was none other than Evangelist Duncan Campbell.

There are times in our life that we need to hear from God or receive direction or spiritual vision. Prayer not only precedes revival, it also precedes vision. The sisters were so moved by this vision that they called for their parish pastor, Rev. James Murray MacKay. Peggy shared the vision and asked Rev.

> **Prayer not only precedes revival, it also precedes vision.**

MacKay to call the leaders of the church to pray as well.

Just two weak sisters, but oh, how powerful in prayer they were. So powerful that their influence led their pastor to call the leaders to prayer as well. These men met in a barn, and alongside the sisters, they prayed for God to awaken the dying church and reach the community. The entire group was burdened by the state of the church. They all saw that church attendance was decreasing, while attendance to the theaters, dance halls, and bars was increasing. They were not just praying for breakthrough; they were literally Praying for Reign, for God's kingdom to invade earth.

REVIVAL COMES

As everyone prayed together—the church, the men in the barn, the two sisters and many others—God came into the Isle of Lewis. Exactly when it started no one knows, but the effects of it touched people everywhere, not just in the church but also in the community. When you read accounts of the Hebrides Revival, you see how God first came into the local church. Many of the remaining church members of the Barvas Free Church were swept up by God's holy conviction, bringing them to a place of deep repentance and rededication. What is most notable about the Hebrides Revival is that it greatly impacted people who weren't even close to a church. It was clear that once the local church was lit on fire, that fire spread to those who did not even attend church. What is amazing is that it didn't spread to the community through a herald or evangelist—it was the sovereign work of God.

DESPERATION FOR GOD

Of the many stories that illustrate this, none are as striking as the story of the young people who were not at the church when God stepped in. They were at a local dance. As the church lost more and more young people, the local attractions and entertainment of the world drew them in instead. However, as revival began to engulf the church in answer to the prayers, it spread into the community and began to pull the youth back to God.

In a very famous account told by Duncan Campbell, the revival was just beginning when several young people who were attending a dance nearby were hit with the power of God. It is almost certain that none of them knew about the prayer meetings at the church. After all, why would they when they no longer attended church? As the story goes, many of those young people at the dance came under the strong conviction of a loving God. The vision Peggy and Christine had was about to become a reality, as the Holy Spirit was working on the hearts of the young people. The conviction was so strong, it caused these young people to seek out some type of help for their lost souls. Can you imagine God working through your prayers so powerfully that people who don't even go to your church are drawn to seek God?

No one is sure why, maybe it was because it was so late at night, but these young people searching for spiritual help ended up at the local police station. I love the eyewitness reports that have been told over and over again through books and Duncan Campbell himself. It records what happened at the very infancy of the revival when, as Duncan Campbell put it, "God stepped down." Have you ever thought of your prayers as a staircase that enables God to step down? If you have not viewed them as such, I would challenge you to do so now.

> **Can you imagine God working through your prayers so powerfully that people who don't even go to your church are drawn to seek God?**

That night, Duncan Campbell dismissed the church meeting at four o'clock in the morning. As he was just dismissing the service, a messenger rushed in and told him that the police were requesting him to come and help several people who were at the station. The person went on to explain that these people were there because they had come under such great conviction that they desperately needed help for their souls. As Duncan Campbell and the others made their way to the station, they found men and women all over the place, on their faces and crying for mercy from God. These were not people who had been at the church meeting; these were people who had been to a dance or elsewhere in the community.

What occurred that would turn a night of revelry into a night of deep soul-searching and spiritual distress? A move of God had arrived, and it began because people were praying. It had come to the Hebrides Islands because two weak sisters had turned their humble cottage into a prayer missile silo, one in which they were used by God to strike down the work of the enemy in their village. Peggy and Christine had power with God in prayer, because they never quit believing that God would honor and use their prayers.

There is no substitute for earnest prayer when it comes to experiencing a move of God. Your prayers, no matter how weak or unimportant you may feel, could be all the difference in seeing a Heaven-sent deluge of His presence in your church and community. If God can use two elderly sisters, one blind and the other lame, then He can use you and me. Let's pray, and keep praying until we hear the reign!

HOW YOU CAN PRAY FOR REIGN IN YOUR CHURCH

Here are eight keys that will help you learn how to be effective in Praying for Reign in your local church.

Begin by asking God for a burden to pray for your church. This may seem very basic, but the truth is that many people do not pray for their church simply because it's not on their heart to do so. While they see the church as a refuge to help meet their own needs, they often fail to realize the important part they have to play. Begin by asking God to give you His heart for your church.

Pray for your pastors and leaders. No one can use your prayers more than the leaders who fight through all kinds of discouragement and attacks while shepherding and leading your congregation. While it's easier for some to criticize than pray, nothing can make more of a difference in the church than dedicated intercessors who will pray for their leaders and their families.

Talk to your pastor. Let your pastor know you are praying for them and their family. While we mostly pray in secret, it can be very helpful to let your pastor know you are praying. First, they will be greatly encouraged. Second, they may let you know some ways you can pray for them and their family specifically. While it takes time to build this prayer trust between an intercessor and their pastor, it always begins with a conversation. Last, they may connect you to other intercessors in the church who are praying as well.

Learn the history of your church. There are tidbits of powerful truth and insight buried in the history of your local church. To find out when and why a church was established is gaining a key understanding that you can carry with you in prayer. For example, you could learn that the founding pastor was given a clear vision of reaching the youth within the community. That when the church was established, the pastor and the congregation prayed for all the schools that were within ten miles of the church. As long as that insight aligns with your current pastor's vision, you can know your prayers are not alone, but are joined to the prayers of past and former members. That is what Dutch Sheets refers to as the "Synergy of the Ages.'" Our prayers being added to their prayers creates powerful synergy.

Get to church early. There is nothing quite as powerful as praying on site. Over the years, I have heard intercessors testify more than once that praying at a specific place gives them insight they would not normally have. You can be powerfully used by just coming to church early, to sit in your chair and pray for the upcoming service. While you may not see any noticeable results from those few extra minutes of prayer, you can know for sure that if God is leading you, it is being effective.

Don't draw attention to yourself. In praying for your church, you may find yourself led to do a few things that may seem unusual to some people. For example, you may find yourself moved to pray over the empty chairs before the service begins. While this is really quite common, and most pastors would gladly welcome it, you still should make sure it's okay with your pastor. The most important thing to remember is that you are not trying to draw attention to yourself; you are trying to draw attention to God through prayer.

Most prophetic revelation is for private intercession, not public input. If you give yourself to sincerely praying for your pastor and church, know that God is going to show you a lot. While many intercessors will immediately see this possible prophetic insight as something they should tell the pastor, more often than not, it's private revelation that they need to take to God in prayer, not the pastor. This is important because if it truly is from God, He will eventually confirm it. More importantly, He'll give the intercessor direction on how to pray about it. For example, you may see the youth coming under some form of spiritual attack. That should be taken to God in prayer for both confirmation and direction. The enemy loves to try and pull intercessors away from where their power lies—in private prayer with God. He most often does it by the temptation to bring forth the revelation into the open in hopes of gaining public approval. We all like to feel good about what we are doing, which makes us all subject to this trickery.

Pray with others. Whether it is with a group of intercessors from the church or it's just other church members, join with others in prayer. When more than one person comes together for prayer, God promises to be in their midst. There is a special power inserted into our prayers when we pray with others. Many churches have found when they make the prayer meeting the most important meeting, God takes care of everything else.

Chapter Six

RIPPLES AT THE WELL

Praying for Reign in Your Job

Therefore, when the Lord knew that the Pharisees had heard that Jesus made and baptized more disciples than John (though Jesus Himself did not baptize, but His disciples), He left Judea and departed again to Galilee. But He needed to go through Samaria. So He came to a city of Samaria which is called Sychar, near the plot of ground that Jacob gave to his son Joseph. Now Jacob's well was there. Jesus therefore, being wearied from *His* journey, sat thus by the well. John 4:1-6

I t's amazing how God will send someone across the world to a mission field in a foreign land, just to extend His kingdom within the borders of that region or country. I also find it amazing how God will send someone into a place of business to accomplish the very same thing. One of the wonderful mysteries of how God works is

> **One of the wonderful mysteries of how God works is how He has a way of directing us to our mission fields, and often it is through our career or chosen field of work.**

how He has a way of directing us to our mission fields, and often it is through our career or chosen field of work.

Too many times people tend to think of work as only a place that we go to just so we can earn enough money to pay our bills, but for the Christian it can be much more than just that. On the other hand, there are people who view work as a chosen career, the fulfilment of a personal dream. Nothing can be better than when we have a job or career that provides a deep personal sense of satisfaction, as though we were made to fulfill that role. It's a wonderful thing about our God, how He can align our desires with His purposes. There are times when He will direct us into a place of work that does not necessarily meet the definition of our dream job, but even then He still has some purpose within it. Sadly, there are also those who see their jobs only as places of great frustration and personal angst. Truly nothing is harder than working a job you despise and hate. No matter how you view your job, God desires for you to find more than just a paycheck or a dream-come-true through your work; He also wants you to find His kingdom through your work.

> No matter how you view your job, God desires for you to find more than just a paycheck or a dream-come-true through your work; He also wants you to find His kingdom through your work.

GOD CREATED WORK

What if I told you that you and I were created to work, that God made us to be those who not only earn a living, but more than that. He created us to create, to be those who contribute. It's an awesome plan that God works out for us to find careers or roles which it feels like we were made to fill. I am so thankful God has put me in many roles where it felt like the position was made for my life, even if it was only for a season. I am also thankful for the jobs that were not my dream job, but provided me with finances my family needed, as well as experience and education that helped me down the road. There are so many wonderful things about working, but there is even more that God has hidden within our jobs. This often-hidden part may be the best part of all: God has hidden ministry within all of our jobs.

WHERE DOES REAL MINISTRY HAPPEN?

Think of how much ministry went on in the Bible at the gates, markets, or gathering places. Think of how much went on at the well. The story in John chapter four of the Samaritan woman at the well is a powerful illustration of this. Jacob's well was much more than a source of water; it was also a gathering place and a workplace. While it was primarily women who went to the well early in the morning to draw water for their household, there were also those who were traveling and stopped there. This would have been a busy gathering point as even those who had livestock went to the well to water their flocks. Today we might think of that well as your workplace or anyplace people go for provision or supply. Just imagine if the Bible was being written today; it might have said that Jesus had to go out of His way to Walmart or He had to stop by the office on His way to church.

> **God has hidden ministry within all of our jobs.**

"Thy kingdom come" is not limited to the church. I think too many times we are held to the belief that the only way to extend the kingdom is to get more people to come to church. While church attendance is very important, God has given us the call to go and take the kingdom to where we live and work. I can already hear some of you saying, "You don't understand, I work in a secular business and there is no way I can bring the kingdom of God into this place." I have news for you: if you work there and you are a born-again,

> **You can and should make a difference where you work, but it has to begin with and be sustained by prayer.**

Christ-following believer, then the kingdom of God has already invaded your work. It invaded it when you were hired. The question now is what you are going to do with it? You can and should make a difference where you work, but it has to begin with and be sustained by prayer. Praying for Reign at work is basically partnering with and agreeing with God through prayer for the fulfillment of His plan to manifest His kingdom realm at your job, just as it is in Heaven.

You might be saying to yourself, "But you don't understand, I work at a bar." While it might not be God's plan for you to stay there long-term, guess what? God just invaded a bar and He did it through you! Once we can understand that God always wants to work through us to impact our places of work, then we can begin to understand the greater purpose of our work. It's not just about paychecks and dreams, it's about working with God in the field–the field of His ever-expanding kingdom.

> **Praying for Reign at work is basically partnering with and agreeing with God through prayer for the fulfillment of His plan to manifest His kingdom realm at your job, just as it is in Heaven.**

THE GATES OF HELL CANNOT WIN AGAINST PRAYER IN THE WORKPLACE

Here is some great news: I have seen God overtake the gates of hell in a neighborhood, and I have seen Him do it in a workplace. God needs pastors, evangelists, teachers, prophets, and apostles in His kingdom but He also needs policemen, football coaches, stay-at-home moms, clerks, loan officers, and on and on.

Have you ever thought that your position could be the bridge that is used by God to take down the gateway of the enemy where you work at? In your job you are not only called to pierce the darkness, you're also called to release light. I know some of you might be thinking right now, "I don't know where you work at, but it would take a miracle to do that in my place of work." Trust me, I have worked in some places that were very difficult, and don't think for a minute that just because it was a "Christian company" that it meant everyone in the company was a Christian or acted like one.

Every job is difficult but every job, if it's the one that God has placed you in, is ripe with incredible opportunities to impact and expand the kingdom. You just need to understand that it must start with and be sustained by prayer. If you are doubtful that is possible, I am going to share how you can begin to influence your place of employment and even your career through the power of prayer. I have not only heard many stories of others who did it, I have seen it happen through my own life as well.

In my time of being a working man I have been everything from a loan officer to a football coach, a state trooper, a pastor and church planter, as well as a manager at a Christian publishing company.

The stories I will tell in this chapter are meant to encourage you to believe that you can and should make a difference at work for the kingdom of God. You are not alone, for God not only goes with you, He also goes before you and prepares the way.

I have seen God use me and use prayer throughout my working career and I have found that there is no gate of hell, not even in the worst business or organization, that can stop God from working there if that is where He is placing you. Even if it's a temporary job, the kind that God is going to remove you from in time, you can still have some type of influence while you are there.

YOUR JOB IS NOT YOUR ENEMY; IT'S YOUR MINISTRY

Too many times, inspired Christians have thought of their place of work as the enemy of God's purposes and calling in their life. I can't tell you how many Christians I have met who have longed to leave their secular or even Christian jobs to enter full-time ministry. They unfortunately thought that the real work of the kingdom was in the church and not the world. Unchecked, their desire for ministry only led to them hating their jobs even more.

This hatred of work would often cause them to make statements like, "If I could only give my whole life to serving God in the ministry, I would truly be happy." Or "Please Lord, open the door to full-time ministry and get me out of this job." I know these statements all too well, for they have been my own statement at one time or another. I must have made statements like that dozens, if not hundreds, of times on my own journey. I remember working with another guy who felt called to the ministry as well. We would talk about our desire to leave our jobs and enter the ministry. We talked about it so much that we both missed many clear opportunities to actually minister to the people around us in the place God had planted us. We missed ministry simply for our desire for the ministry.

I have not been the only one who has worshipped the ministry, thinking it would be so much more fulfilling than my secular job. I have met many others who could not see the God-ordained potential for kingdom influence and impact right in the midst of their occupation. Back then I thought I just needed to be delivered from my job, but God was about to deliver me from my view of my job. He was getting ready to open the doors wide to ministry and teach me about the power of prayer at the work place.

HOW GOD DELIVERED ME

When I was a state trooper in the late 80's, this desire to leave the patrol and become a minister had hit a fever pitch. I was very involved in the church we attended, even leading the college and career ministry. In my plan, I would use my off-duty time to study and work toward obtaining my credentials for ministry. I was very driven, mainly by the fact that this would be my ticket out of the patrol and into the ministry. During this time, I would not only dream about becoming a pastor, I worshipped it. I thought becoming a pastor was the key to my future happiness. Thankfully God had another plan.

Have you ever felt like you were in a job that seemed to be blocking you from God's plan for your life? That's how I felt, and the more I thought about it the more miserable I became. Going to work was becoming more than just a chore; it was becoming my enemy.

I spent three years trying to leave the patrol, only to hear the Lord instead tell me to leave my pursuit of ministry and just go back to being a good state trooper. Have you ever worked for something for years to only have it blocked off? It's one thing if it's a person or circumstances blocking you; it's a whole other thing if it's God. Thankfully I have learned to trust the voice of God and even when it doesn't make sense I (eventually) am going to follow His voice.

I then turned my pursuit of ministry into the pursuit of fulfilling my role as a state trooper with excellence. I determined to start each day with prayer, asking the Lord to guide my daily tasks. Day in and day out I heard, "Write tickets and do a great job." I heard this for maybe ten months (though it seemed like ten years) until one day I heard something different.

God answered my prayer with, "Today you will pray with a couple on the side of the road." That was new! Up until that moment it had been all about just doing the job I was hired to do. Several hours later, I found an older couple on the side of the road with a flat tire. The little old lady was so excited to see me when I drove up behind their old Buick. She quickly told me about their flat tire and asked me if I would contact AAA for them. I said I'd be glad to, and since AAA was right down the road it wouldn't take them long to get here. It was in that moment I heard the Lord say to me, "You change their tire."

There is nothing I hate more than changing a tire. I mean, I have thrown my back out several times just trying to get the tire out of the trunk! But God had spoken, so I told the lady I'd change the tire. She tried to convince me to just call AAA, but she had no idea I was under orders from a higher authority. I noticed her husband sitting in the passenger seat with his legs out on the ground and a cane in his right hand. It was clear she was the one driving.

As I changed their tire, I asked where they were headed. She said, "Shand's Hospital to see a specialist about my husband's heart condition." Apparently, he was in very poor health and needed a miracle. I knew then this was the couple God directed me to pray with. As I finished changing the tire, the lady offered me twenty-five dollars for helping. I thanked her but told her it was my job to help, and that I couldn't take her money. She smiled and put the money back into her purse. I went on, "While I can't take your money, there is one thing you could do for me. Would you allow me to pray for you and your husband?" She answered, "Yes." And then she started to cry. I prayed one of the shortest, simplest prayers I've ever prayed, but I could feel the power in every word. When I finished, she hugged and thanked me. She said, "We had a word from God that someone would pray with us along the way to Gainesville and that God would heal my husband. You were that person. Thank you!"

You see, Jesus needed to go through Samaria because there was a woman there who needed to be restored and needed to meet God. I needed to go to the Florida Turnpike because there was a woman there who needed someone to pray with her and her husband so he could be healed.

Have you ever thought of your job as a well? A place where people gather and come together for all kinds of reasons? Some come to work, some come to buy, some come to watch and others come just to gather with people. The lost and hurting are not gathering at churches or houses of worship; they are gathering at wells.

> **The lost and hurting are not gathering at churches or houses of worship; they are gathering at wells.**

They are where you work at, and that is even if you work in a Christian company.

As that couple drove off, I sat in my patrol car and took in what had just happened. I was still for an hour or so, with thought after thought tumbling through my brain as I came to grips with what God was doing. I heard the voice of the Lord as He spoke to my heart and said these words: "I can give you a church to pastor, or I can give you the whole turnpike to pastor. What do you want?"

That encounter was the beginning of many open doors for ministry and scores of stories and testimonies of answered prayer while I was a state trooper. It even led to the start of a group called Troopers for Christ.

While there were two or three other Christian troopers who wanted to gather weekly for prayer, the majority of those I worked with never expressed an interest. While I'm not suggesting they were not followers of Christ, as most of the officers I worked with were really good men and women that expressed a belief in God, there was just no established prayer gathering or prayer groups. Honestly, I was not expecting one when I came to work, but God had a plan and it involved me being a key influence to help establish it.

There is nothing easy about being an influence for Christ in the midst of a very tough work environment. The people I worked with were underpaid, overworked, and many had both personal and relational challenges. Sadly, too many people try to paint law enforcement officers as bad people because of one or two bad officers. The vast majority of them are not people who wake up every day ready to arrest someone; they are good people who want to help others. I only ran across one or two like that during my time as a state trooper, but I met many who were guarded, closed off, and dealing with both the stresses of life and a difficult job. The divorce rate is high in law enforcement for a reason. It's a very tough job. We need to pray for the many men and women who serve us and our communities in this underpaid and sometimes underappreciated profession.

MY JACOB'S WELL

How do you feel about your job now? Does it feel like a destiny or a dungeon?

I knew in my twenties God was directing me to become a state trooper, but I thought it was just a job until I could get my credentials for ministry. In my plans, as soon as I received my license to preach, I would surely be joining the staff at my church or somewhere. I really thought I would only be in law enforcement for a few years—not for almost fifteen.

Without me knowing it, God had directed me to my own "Jacob's well." As I ministered to a fellow trooper who had been married at least five times, I realized there was need all around me. Looking back on it, I remember thinking, "How am I going to make a difference in the middle of closed, suspicious hearts and high stress, especially when I was hired to write tickets and work wrecks, not lead a ministry?" That is the question I want to answer

How do you feel about your job now? Does it feel like a destiny or a dungeon?

for all of you. How can you impact and influence the people you work with for Christ? The answer is prayer, and it's absolutely essential to not only start it, but also sustain it. I will say this about prayer and work; it is virtually impossible to be an influence for Christ in your job without prayer. I also want to encourage you that no matter where you work or how hard the environment is, God can use you to influence people and impact change for His kingdom. You just need to remember that man may have hired you, but God ultimately positions you. Work as though you are working for God, and pray as if it all depends on Him.

HOW TO PRAY FOR REIGN AT WORK

Here are six keys to help you effectively Pray for Reign at your job.

Talk to God about your job: At the end of the day, God created work, not man. He understands more about your job and the people you work with than anyone else does. Think of God as the HR Manager over your job. You can talk to Him about anything involving your work and He will have the answer for you. Most of all, ask Him to give you a

> **Man may have hired you, but God ultimately positions you. Work as though you are working for God.**

heart for the work and for the people. You can refuse to ask Him, but in the end, it will only get worse and not better. Listen to this lesson I learned about asking for God's help in a tough job.

Years later, after I had transitioned into full-time ministry, we were moving back to Florida from Texas to plant a new church in Winter Springs, Florida. (You can read more about that adventure in my first book, *Respond Up.*) After we returned, I needed to find a job to help support us while we planted the church. The only job I could find was at Chase Bank, in the credit card division. I was a service-to-sales advisor.

My job was simple: address your question or need, then sell you one of our products. I really hated the job in the beginning and I thought often of quitting. *Why did God bring me to this place? How long would I have to serve there?* It wasn't until I asked God my favorite question that I got an answer:

"God, what do you want me to do?"

"Don, I want you to ask Me to bless you at Chase."

I remember thinking, "I don't want to be blessed here, I want to leave here." No matter what I said or thought, those were the final instructions from God.

After a few days, I finally stopped fighting God's plan and I started resting in God. I asked Him to bless me and make me a great salesperson with lots of sales. I'd love to tell you it was easy, but I would be lying to you and everyone else reading this book. It did, however, became easier each day when I prayed that same prayer as I parked my car. A year after that prayer, I had gone from being at the bottom of the sales ladder to winning the award for the top salesperson in my entire division. I went on to win the same award again the next year.

You may be resistant to talking to God about your job, but it's not going to get any better until you do. Who knows what opportunity you may be missing simply because you may be afraid to ask Him for help. God not only blessed me by making me the top sales person, He also opened up a lot of favor to share His love with my coworkers. The blessing He brought helped my paycheck, but it also helped me connect with others as I shared what I was learning on my way to the top. There is no platform for ministry greater than the one God can create for you at work.

The biggest change is that I went from hating my job to loving my job, but it all began when I talked to God about my role and obeyed what He directed me to do.

Pray before work, while at work and after work. We've already talked about how prayer is more about God getting our attention than us getting His. The question you need to ask God is, "What do you want me to pray for at work?" God will either answer you, teach you, or show you what or who to pray for. You may be the only person at that plant or office who is engaged in prayer but that is exactly why you are there, so pray. Whatever God opens up, it will be because you started a prayer meeting with just you and Him. You plus God is always a majority. You can walk through the office, praying over each desk and chair without anyone but you and God knowing that you are praying.

Never wait for a prayer meeting to be established; start one with just you and God. If there is one, I would encourage you to join and support it even if those believers are from a different denomination or background.

Do a good job. Nothing can discredit a Christian at work more than being a lazy or distracted worker. It's important that they see you do your job and do it well. It's not important that they see you pray and read your Bible or that you have a fish sticker on your car. Co-workers see Christ in an employee first through things like work ethic, kindness, honesty, patience, and compassion. I have been able to pray for hours in some of my jobs while doing the best job I could have done, and no one ever knew I was even in prayer. It's important that they know excellence in my life before they hear grandeur in my prayers. In the end, I pray before my Father in Heaven, but I work before my co-workers on earth.

Take the lesson of Joseph from the book of Genesis. No matter where he went, in forced service to Potiphar or wrongfully placed in prison, he did a good job and was always promoted. The beginning of power in prayer at work is always linked to faithfulness in your job, especially the small things. If you will be faithful in the little things, like helping and encouraging your co-workers daily, God will not only give you favor but also more authority and influence.

Ask God to connect you with others in your office who pray. While you can pray alone, it is powerful when God connects you to other believers with whom you work. Even if you consider them to be weaker in faith or they come from a different denominational viewpoint than yours, you should be open to connecting to them for prayer, encouragement, and friendship. Asking God to connect you to those who also believe is a very important request. Trust me, it may take a while, but He will lead you. God may even prompt you to start a lunchtime prayer meeting that you share on a company bulletin board. Each workplace is uniquely different so what may work for one person may not work for another. The important thing is to ask God to lead you by His Holy Spirit. While you do not know who may or may not follow Christ, God knows. Just ask Him in prayer and He will lead you and eventually connect you with other believers.

Work within the rules of your company, but believe God will create a space for you. It's important that you work within the rules of your company. They may not allow anyone to meet in the break area or post things on the bulletin board. Take the steps God ordains and go through the doors He opens. For years I started and led a prayer time during lunch. There was no room in the office to accommodate our group, as meetings were taken place throughout the day in the conference room. The small group I was leading had no choice but find another location to pray in. We eventually found a picnic table outside of our office building underneath some trees. Before long, other people from our office asked if they could meet us at the picnic table and pray during lunch. We slowly grew from three to seven faithful prayer warriors. That picnic table became a cherished place of prayer. Why? Because we were honoring our company rules and God had a special place. I still go to that table sometimes to pray and remember that special season in my journey in prayer.

Expect warfare. As I've said: prayer is not magic; prayer is warfare. Seasoned prayer warriors understand prayer can take time and effort, sometimes without seeing any results for a long time. That is because prayer is powerful and the enemy hates it and will do everything he can to resist it and stop it. I have come under major attack when I pray, but especially when I have prayed at work. Praying at work, for others or for the company, is taking the prayer battle to the gates of hell. Imagine if every Christ-follower in America would truly engage the gates of hell in their workplace through the power of prayer. What would happen? I think a great revival would break out across the land, but it wouldn't start at the church building. It would start at the church at the office. It would start at the well.

One of the most important things to remember is this: at work you will either take ground, or the ground will try to take you. If you are working someplace where you are the only light, just know if you fail to pray and attempt to open the door of the kingdom of God into your workplace, the enemy will in turn work to open the door of darkness into your life. Be a light! Even if you are the only one praying and no one knows you are praying. Yes, the enemy will work against your prayers the best he can, but he can only do so much when God is leading you. And he will

> **At work you will either take ground, or the ground will try to take you.**

not be able to tempt you to enter into the things he is doing there. A Christian who prays for his co-workers is less likely to enter into destructive gossip than one who never prays.

Over the years I have seen firsthand how the power of prayer can invade the workplace and literally change the people and even the culture of the company. During my time as a state trooper, I observed some of the most impossible people and situations change, and it all came through the doorway of prayer. No matter where you work, you may not be able to witness or talk about your faith, but you are absolutely able to pray. Pray for Reign at work and watch what God does as His kingdom begins to come into your job. The gates of hell cannot prevail against your prayers at work.

Chapter Seven

IT'S ALL ABOUT THE TREES

Praying for Reign in Your Family

The Spirit of the Lord God is upon Me,
Because the Lord has anointed Me
To preach good tidings to the poor;
He has sent Me to heal the brokenhearted,
To proclaim liberty to the captives,
And the opening of the prison to those who are bound;
To proclaim the acceptable year of the Lord,
And the day of vengeance of our God;
To comfort all who mourn,
To console those who mourn in Zion,
To give them beauty for ashes,
The oil of joy for mourning,
The garment of praise for the spirit of heaviness;
That they may be called trees of righteousness,
The planting of the Lord, that He may be glorified.
Isaiah 61:1-3

Over the years, it seems the prayer request I receive the most is to pray for someone's family. It can be a request to pray for a marriage on the rocks, or it can be a request to pray for God to heal an aging parent. There are all kinds of prayer requests for members of one's family because that is the first church anyone is a part of: The First Church of The Family. It's what touches and moves all of us well before the needs of foreign missions or international issues that cause us fear.

A DAUGHTER'S LIFE SAVED

This "family first" reality reminds me of one of the most miraculous answers to prayer I have ever witnessed. Years ago, one of my co-workers came to pull me out of a meeting because someone in our company had just received tragic news. This employee had received a text from their daughter saying that she wanted to say goodbye to him, as she was about to take her own life. Obviously, this father attempted to call her immediately, but his calls went to voicemail. To make matters worse, his daughter was hundreds of miles away and he had no idea where she could be, so he couldn't direct the police to any location to help her. There is no doubt this man felt totally helpless. You could see both his desperation and how hopeless he felt in his tears. No other prayer request mattered at this point.

Have you ever felt like this man did? Desperately wanting God to intervene in the life of a loved one? I think of the stories in the Bible, like the story of Jairus who desperately needed a miracle for his daughter:

> Now when Jesus had crossed over again by boat to the other side, a great multitude gathered to Him; and He was by the sea. And behold, one of the rulers of the synagogue came, Jairus by name. And when he saw Him, he fell at His feet and begged Him earnestly, saying, "My little daughter lies at the point of death. Come and lay Your hands on her, that she may be healed, and she will live." Mark 5:21-23

There is nothing the majority of us won't do when it comes to getting help for our children or a loved one. All throughout scripture, you can read stories that illustrate how important family is and how much we will work to find help for those we love most. Like the story of Jairus, my friend at work was desperate for help for his daughter, and that meant interrupting a meeting.

> **There is nothing the majority of us won't do when it comes to getting help for our children or a loved one.**

As I made my way out of the meeting, I was directed to a vacant office where I found my friend surrounded by two or three coworkers. I will never forget when he showed me the text and shared how he'd called everyone and did not know what else to do. He was truly desperate for an answer, and the only answer at this point was to pray.

While prayer was already happening when I came into the room, everyone was looking to me, not only to bring but also help lead it. I don't remember what I prayed, but I remember who I was praying to. I was praying to God, and it was in the name of Jesus. I also remember asking the Holy Spirit, our prayer partner, to lead us. They were looking for me to lead the prayer, but I was looking for the Holy Spirit to lead me.

As we prayed and asked for God's help for my friend's daughter, I began to see a picture in my heart. It was a picture of a wooded area near a river. It would not go away, so I asked my friend, "Is there anywhere near where your daughter lives that is like a park? Or a wooded area that is near a river?" He quickly grabbed his phone which had a map pulled up on it. He pointed to a park area that was close to where his daughter lived.

> **They were looking for me to lead the prayer, but I was looking for the Holy Spirit to lead me.**

I really did not know for sure where she was, but I did know that we had asked the Holy Spirit to lead us and if He was leading, I was going to follow. I said, "I just feel that she could be in that area. We need to pray the police find her; that they are directed to where she is at." We prayed for about fifteen minutes, asking the Holy Spirit to guide the officers to that location, that if she was really there, it would be made known.

After that, my friend made his way to the airport because either way he was flying to that city. Several of us continued to pray. I think it was about thirty minutes later he called me, sobbing on the other end of the phone, saying they found his daughter and had found her in time to rush her to the hospital to save her life. Where did they find her? They found her in those woods by the river. They actually used her cell phone signal to pinpoint where she was, but according to the police, if they had been five minutes later, it would not have turned out like it did.

While I have heard many other miraculous answers to prayer for family members, this one put a permanent mark within my soul. While we aren't guaranteed to have every desperate situation work out like my friend's did, we still have a present help for any time of trouble, especially for those times that involve our family.

THE ENEMY'S PLAN TO HINDER PRAYER FOR OUR FAMILY

The enemy hates when we pray for our families. He knows the authority we have when we pray with our spouse or when we pray for our children and grandchildren. This is the reason he will do anything to stop someone from praying for (or with) their family. If you would like to see how Satan works to hinder prayer for the family, you have to go back to the beginning. Back to the garden with Adam and Eve.

When you look at the story of Adam and Eve in detail, you can see the MO of the enemy. (What does MO stand for? MO stands for "modus operandi," which is a Latin term.) This term is used a lot in law enforcement, as it typically describes the way a person or group operates. It's a way of describing their typical behavior or routine of operation. We know the MO of how our enemy works because it is laid in God's work. The MO of the enemy is to lie.

FOUR LIES THE ENEMY USES TO STOP US FROM PRAYING FOR OUR FAMILIES

Lie Number One: Prayer does not work. The enemy loves to tell us that prayer for our family does not work. He will begin by saying things like, "Look at what happened last time you prayed…nothing!" As he works to remind you of every failed prayer request, the goal is to stop your prayers by robbing your belief. For example, you may be on your second marriage, and now you are having issues in your current relationship. While you should strongly consider getting counseling for your marriage, you should never give in to his attacks on your confidence in prayer.

Just because prayer did not work in a previous situation or did not work for your friend, that does not mean prayer does not work. Great, seasoned prayer warriors have all experienced unanswered prayers, or prayers that were not answered in the way or the time frame they desired. Don't allow the enemy to take what appears to be one or two losses and cause you to quit believing in the power of prayer. Remind yourself daily of God's promise in the book of James:

> Confess and acknowledge how you have offended one another and then pray for one another to be instantly healed, for tremendous power is released through the passionate, heartfelt prayer of a godly believer! Elijah was a man with human frailties, just like all of us, but he prayed and received supernatural answers. He actually shut the heavens over the land so there would be no rain for three and a half years! Then he prayed again and the skies opened up over the land so that the rain came again and produced the harvest. James 5:16-18 (TPT)

Don't believe the lies of the enemy, even if you deal with doubt. I have heard it said before that we need to "doubt our doubts, and believe our beliefs." The enemy works on our mind to try to get us to doubt our beliefs and to believe our doubts. As long as we are alive on this earth we will have to battle doubt. It just comes with the territory, especially when praying for family.

Lie Number Two: You don't have the authority. As a Christian, you have great authority when it comes to praying for your family. This is especially true if you are a Christian parent. As a parent, you have been given incredible authority to pray for your family. All throughout Scripture, we can read about how a parent's life can either pass blessing onto their child or curses. The fact that those two results are possible means that parents have the authority to influence their children for good or bad. Satan knows that we have that God-given authority so he works to attack it through two of his greatest weapons: deception and condemnation.

> **Don't allow the enemy to take what appears to be one or two losses and cause you to quit believing in the power of prayer.**

Deception: Notice the very subtle trickery of Satan when he says to Eve, "For God knows that in the day you eat of it your eyes will be opened, and you will be like God, knowing good and evil" (Genesis 3:5). What is crazy is this: Adam and Eve were already like God. They were made in His image and likeness, but the enemy was able to plant the seed of doubt by suggesting that if Eve took of the forbidden fruit, then she and Adam would be like God. This is deception and it's a trick of the enemy where he works to create doubt in who we really are. He will try to do the same with you, especially when it comes to praying for your family.

Condemnation: The next weapon of the enemy is condemnation. He will tell you that you don't deserve help with your marriage or family, so you shouldn't ask. He'll try to convince you that you do not warrant help from God; he will hold up your past or even recent failures to convince you to disqualify yourself. He will try to get you bound by the trauma of your past in hopes that this will make you feel like God won't hear your prayers because of your failure.

While it's true that unrepented sin can block your prayers, once you have repented and accepted the grace and forgiveness of God, you have been restored to your position as a son or daughter. In God's process of restoring us back to our kingdom authority, there is no penalty box we have to sit in until we have learned our lesson. If that was true, then when the prodigal son returned home, the father would have not said:

> In God's process of restoring us back to our kingdom authority, there is no penalty box we have to sit in until we have learned our lesson.

> Bring out the best robe and put *it* on him, and put a ring on his hand and sandals on *his* feet. And bring the fatted calf here and kill *it*, and let us eat and be merry; for this my son was dead and is alive again; he was lost and is found. Luke 15:22-24

If he had to wait on having his authority restored, the father would have said instead, "Set him up a cot in the servant's quarters and put him to work in the fields. Let him earn his way back into the family."

While the robe represents that he was totally accepted with no need for a visit to the penalty box, it's the ring that really stands out when it comes to us being restored to kingdom authority in prayer. In ancient times, there was great significance when a ring was given to someone, especially a son. It meant more than just acceptance; it meant the granting of authority to the son. The father putting his ring on the prodigal son was a way of giving the son his full authority back to serve as a co-operator with his father. When the enemy tries to tell you that you are disqualified, hold up the ring of son-ship or daughter-ship.

Lie Number Three: You can't pray for this; you caused it. The enemy will try to say that you have no right to pray for a situation because you personally caused it. He will use this argument against people who have failed in their marriages, but they are praying for it to be restored. This also happens a lot with parents who failed to be a good parent at some point or another. The enemy simply points to the results of our failed attempts at parenting and says, "If you would have been a better parent, this would have never happened. I guess you are now praying for a crop failure." While there is bitter truth in the fact that we do reap what we sow, there is a more powerful truth which trumps that one every time. That truth is called the mercy and grace of God.

> **Mercy is not getting what you really deserve.** You may deserve the conflict in your marriage or the rebellious rejection of your children, but thank God for mercy.

> **Grace is getting what you really do not deserve.** You may not deserve a restored marriage or harmony in your family, but through Christ, God's grace has been extended to you.

Because of these two special gifts from God, you can respond to the enemy's lies in confidence. You can say, "I may have caused this, and I may be reaping what I have sown, but God has extended His mercy and grace to me so I can pray for this."

While there definitely needs to be repentance and possible restitution, you need to know that you can pray for healing and restoration. In the end, you will need God's help to make the first step in rebuilding your marriage or family, so don't let this lie stop you from asking God for help. If you have repented and asked for God's grace and forgiveness to be appropriated into your life then you now have full authority to stand before the Father in prayer. Again, when the enemy brings up the lie that you caused it so you can't pray for help, just show him your robe and your ring.

WHAT I HAVE LEARNED ABOUT PRAYER

I have learned a lot about prayer in my lifetime, and much of it from teachers who taught and wrote on prayer but are no longer with us. I am grateful for people like E.M. Bounds, George Mueller, Rees Howells, and Dr. Myles Monroe. There are also many living generals who have influenced me. People like Dutch Sheets and Cindy Jacobs. Through all of these leaders I have discovered two big truths that shine out regarding prayer. Prayer works but we often fail to work prayer.

Prayer works, but we often fail to work prayer.

GREAT-GREAT-AUNT EPSIE

While I have learned so much from the many generals of prayer who have influenced me, no one has influenced my prayer life like my great-great-aunt Epsie McKay. Aunt Epsie and her husband Clarence McKay were Nazarene ministers who planted and led churches all around the south, but mainly in Florida and Louisiana. He was known as a great preacher, and she was known as a true prayer warrior.

Even though I have no memory of meeting her or my Uncle Clarence, her influence runs very deep within me, especially when it comes to prayer. Early on I can remember being told stories of how fervently she would pray, often getting on her knees. My mother shared with me more than once how she remembers visiting Aunt Epsie and Uncle Clarence when she was a little girl and seeing them lead prayer meetings downstairs. The two-story house that Uncle Clarence and

Aunt Epsie lived in also acted as the church. It was used until a church building could be acquired. They had powerful prayer meetings in that house, and they continued even after they had moved the church into a building. I have been told that they had "prayer kneelers" built all around the living room not only to provide a specific space for prayer but also a little comfort for someone to seek Heaven from their knees. Can you imagine if we had as many specific places to pray in our homes as we have for televisions? To Aunt Epsie and Uncle Clarence, it didn't matter if the church met in their house or not; their home was always a church.

The stories of how Aunt Epsie prayed are so moving to me. There is even one of her going to visit death row to pray with an inmate before he was executed. I've been told that she would pray for anyone anywhere because she believed so strongly in the power of prayer.

One of my favorite stories is how she prayed for my grandfather, who was her niece's husband. My real grandfather unfortunately was not a Christian; in fact, he was very lost and an alcoholic. He and my grandmother became divorced early on in their marriage, leaving my grandmother to raise my mother and her two sisters alone.

Aunt Epsie most certainly had a burden to pray for her whole family, but she had a specific call from God to pray Heaven down for my grandparents. As my mother shares, her great aunt would not give up praying for both her mother and especially for her lost and sick father. I have the Bible that Aunt Epsie gave to my grandmother in 1939. She wrote in the front of it, "May this book teach you the way of life." It was just a small part of her spiritual love and care as she continued to fill the bowls of Heaven over this broken family. For her, no member of her family was ever going to be untouched by the power of God.

Her prayers for my grandparents continued until her death, and she did not leave this world before she visited my grandfather in the hospital and led him to Christ before he passed away. It took over thirty years of praying, but her prayers were answered in the last hours of his life. The influence of Great Aunt Epsie not only moved into my grandmother's life, it moved into my mother's and eventually into mine. My grandmother kept and read that Bible the rest of her life and it was eventually given to me after I preached at my grandmother's funeral.

Not only do I have Aunt Epsie's Bible, I have all of Uncle Clarence's preaching notes. Her Bible sits by my grandmother's on my bookshelf. They are a spiritual treasure to me, but more than that, they are a reminder of the power of prayer when it comes to praying for your family. I recently drove my mother to visit Uncle Clarence and Aunt Epsie's grave. As we stood there reminiscing and recounting the stories of these spiritual pioneers, my mother spoke to the grave as though she was talking directly to Aunt Epsie. She said, "Thank you for praying for momma and daddy." She then said to me, "I still feel her prayers." If you want to know how powerful praying for one's own family can be, just imagine that one day, like my Aunt Epsie, you could have a great-great-grandson or future descendant who stands in front of your grave thanking God for your prayers and influence. In the kingdom, it's all about the trees. It's all about your tree. As we Pray for Reign in our families, we are extending the kingdom of God into the future branches of our tree, ones that will grow out long after you have left this earth for Heaven. It begins with you, and it begins today.

Why do you think some fail to do the one thing that could make the biggest difference, especially when it comes to family? Some have said it's because we are lazy and real prayer takes more work than we are willing to put in. That can be true of some, but a lot of Christians I know are willing to work hard, especially when it comes to family.

Others have said it's not a lack of work ethic; it's a lack of perseverance. We might start out strong, but it only lasts for so long. There is no doubt that to be really effective in prayer we need to learn how to persevere. I know of several stories (and I am sure you do too) where someone prayed for twenty-five years or more to see results in a loved one or family member. So, if it is perseverance that is missing, what are we doing or not doing to not have it? To understand this better, I think we have to go back to the beginning, back to Genesis.

IT'S ALL ABOUT THE TREES

The reason I know it's all about the trees is because of an illustration God showed me earlier in my walk with Him. It was June 5th, 1989; I was sitting at Wekiva Springs Park praying about evangelism and leading people to Christ.

As I was looking at all of the beautiful, majestic oak trees all over the park while watching the people enjoy the springs, the Lord said to me, "Do you see the people who have come here today? Each person is like one of these priceless oak trees. They are like the oaks planted in my plantation, and they are all priceless to me. They are priceless, but Satan does not want me to have them, so he comes to saw them down to destroy them. See the potential in every man and woman, Don; lead them to me."

When I first received this word from God in 1989, I thought it was focusing on just the individual people; a single man or woman. I saw my calling into ministry and evangelism to be leading as many of them to Christ as possible, thus preserving another priceless oak for God. That was how I saw it until God showed me something about trees.

What was missing was that the foundation of this calling was not about one single person, but also the generations who would come after that person. Think about it. In each tree, there are thousands of acorns—and each one of those acorns can each produce a tree of their own. Those trees, when fully developed, will do likewise, and the cycle repeats over and over again. But if you destroy a tree before it produces any acorns, you not only kill that tree but all of the future trees that would come from it. That's why for God, it's all about the trees: it's all about the generations.

PRAYING FOR THE GENERATIONS

God not only taught me a very valuable lesson for evangelism through that story, but He also began to teach me about prayer and how powerful it can be not only to influence your life, but also the lives of your family, both current and future generations. I started to realize through that illustration of the tree that the enemy is not after me alone. He is also after my children and grandchildren. He is after the generational line. In Exodus, the Lord makes it very clear how the generations can be impacted and influenced.

> Now the LORD descended in the cloud and stood with him there, and proclaimed the name of the LORD. And the LORD passed before him and proclaimed, "The LORD, the LORD God, merciful and gracious, longsuffering, and abounding in goodness and truth, keeping mercy for thousands, forgiving iniquity and transgression and sin, by no means clearing the guilty, visiting the iniquity of the fathers upon the children and the children's children to the third and the fourth generation." Exodus 34:5-7

The enemy tries to lie to me and discourage me from praying for my family because he knows the potential that is possible when my children have a godly father who will pray for them. Opposite of the curse is the blessing. Here God promises the blessing will go on and on, to the thousandth generation. The blessing has always been greater than the curse.

HOW YOU CAN PRAY FOR REIGN IN YOUR FAMILY

Here are six keys to help you effectively Pray for Reign in your family.

Begin Early. You can pray for them before they are even conceived. Prayers are eternal, and because that is true, I pray for my great-great-grandkids and even their descendants. I like to call this "praying up the tree."

Pray with your spouse and family. "The family that prays together stays together." While this does not have to be formal, rigid, or stuffy, prayer within the family is a key cornerstone to having the blessing of God upon your home and family.

Pray over your children while they sleep. While it's great to pray over your children while they are standing in front of you, you can really get into some deep and effective prayer while they sleep. No matter if you are rocking them to sleep or just standing at the foot of their bed, praying over them while they sleep is a beautiful gift from God for every parent.

Pray the Word of God over your family. There are few things as powerful as praying God's Word over your marriage or children. I have stood in prayer for my children at different points in their life, using one or two promises from scripture. It's easy to do, all you have to do is substitute their name into the verse or portion of scripture. I love to pray the twenty-third Psalm over my kids: "The LORD *is* _____ shepherd; ____ shall not want" (Psalm 23:1).

Pray for future generations. Pray not just for your kids, but also for your grandchildren and those that will follow them. Dr. James Dobson tells an amazing story[8] of how his own great-grandfather, George McCluskey, prayed for his family every day from eleven in the morning until noon. He not only prayed for his family, but he also prayed for his future generations. Later in George's life, he revealed that God had promised him that if he would pray for his family every day, every member of his family to four generations would become Christians. God kept that promise and as Dr. Dobson has shared, every family member of the family was a Christian to the fourth generation.

Never ever give up. The last but most important thing we should do when Praying for Reign for our families is simple: never quit. While we would all love to see our prayers answered quickly, some prayer requests can take years. No matter what you do, never ever give up praying for your spouse, children, or grandchildren (really for any person). I know a story of a woman who prayed for her husband to be saved for well over twenty-five years. Year after year she prayed, but nothing ever happened. It was only after his death that she learned someone had led him to the Lord hours before he was killed in a tragic car accident. How many times in scripture have we seen a promise take years before it became a reality? You may have prayed for your kids for years and nothing ever happened, but God is not finished. They may be adults now with kids of their own, but it's not time to quit praying. Remember: it's all about the trees.

Chapter Eight

THE MYSTERY OF 412:

Praying for Reign in America

T he whole purpose for writing this book was to encourage the everyday Christian never to underestimate the power of prayer in their lives. While this is true for praying for things close to you, your church, your place of employment, and your family, it is also true for praying for something that is much more vast, as in praying for our nation. God called me to write this book primarily for Christians who call America their home, But these truths can absolutely translate to Christians around the world.

AMERICA IS IN NEED OF AN AWAKENING

Anyone who is over the age of forty has seen America change greatly. I will not even list all of the changes since the early eighties, but America is in a much different place than when Lee Greenwood first sang "God Bless the USA." America was not perfect in the eighties, but it's been on a forty-year journey that has taken it even further away from the

America may have lost her way over the last forty years, but she has not lost her destiny. God still has a plan.

101

biblical foundations it was founded upon. The good news is America may have lost her way over the last four decades, but she has not lost her destiny. God still has a plan.

THERE IS A DIVINE PURPOSE
IN ALL THIS SHAKING

On the morning of June 11th, 2019, I was spending time with the Lord in prayer. This was a very sweet time, as His presence was clearly present and active. As I wrote in my journal that morning, I became aware that God was drawing me deeper in my calling to pray for America.

During this powerful time of prayer, the Holy Spirit led me to a portion of scripture found toward the end of the twelfth chapter of the book of Hebrews. As I read the twenty-fifth verse from the New King James Version, it became clear to me that God was preparing to say something significant.

> See that you do not refuse Him who speaks. For if they did not escape who refused Him who spoke on earth, much more shall we not escape if we turn away from Him who speaks from heaven. Hebrews 12:25

Have you ever had one of those times where you just knew that He was about to speak? This was one of those times for me. I thought, "How important it is to listen for the voice of God! It's everything." As I continued to read, I had a strong desire to move to The Passion Translation for the remainder of the chapter.

> The earth was rocked at the sound of his voice from the mountain, but now he has promised, "Once and for all I will not only shake the systems of the world, but also the unseen powers in the heavenly realm!" Now

this phrase "once and for all" clearly indicates the final removal of things that are shaking, that is, the old order, so only what is unshakable will remain. Since we are receiving our rights to an unshakable kingdom we should be extremely thankful and offer God the purest worship that delights his heart as we lay down our lives in absolute surrender, filled with awe. For our God is a holy, devouring fire! Hebrews 12:26-29 (TPT)

Reading the final few verses in The Passion Translation stirred me deeply. As I meditated on it, God began to speak to me about America and His unshakable kingdom. Without me fully realizing it, these five verses were painting a prophetic picture of what was about to occur over the next few years. No one could ever have predicted or imagined the Covid-19 pandemic nor the civil unrest that would break out just after the pandemic began. When you add to all of that the presidential election of 2020, and other world events that followed like the war in Ukraine, there is no doubt that things have been shaking. It seems like everything that can be shaken is being shaken, but if we believe His Word something incredible can begin to form out of this time, an unshakable kingdom.

THE QUESTION WE ALL NEED TO ANSWER

This portion of scripture has become key to helping me understand what Praying for Reign is all about, especially when it comes to praying for America through these difficult times. As God began to give me an understanding of how He was calling me to pray through the shaking and what waited on the other side, I not only grew in hope, I also gained direction. I learned that Praying for Reign in America means partnering and agreeing with God through prayer for the fulfillment of His plan—His plan to manifest His kingdom realm in America as it is in Heaven. The shaking is obviously being used as part of the plan as well, but what is our part to play? How are we to pray through the shaking to help fulfill His plan for America?

AN INCREDIBLE ENCOUNTER
WITH A VERY OLD SHIP

As I continued my time of prayer that morning on June 11th, I decided to receive communion as part of my prayer time. I often take communion as part of my time since there is nothing like connecting to God through the elements of communion. There truly is *communion* in the communion.

When I had finished receiving communion, a picture of an old ship came to my heart. If you have never had a vision from the Lord before, you know they can come in all kinds of ways. It could be something you actually see or it could be something that you just receive, like a downloaded file. No matter how God does it, it's a blessing to have a Heavenly Father who wants to communicate with us so much that He will use almost anything.

Praying for Reign in America is partnering with and agreeing with God through prayer for the fulfillment of His plan— His plan to manifest His kingdom realm in America as it is in Heaven.

I could tell that this picture was not just my imagination as the detail was very specific and it was not in line with anything I had been thinking about. The ship in the picture was one like the Pilgrims used when they first came to America; one with a large mast and several sails attached to it. In this picture, the ship was forging ahead, crashing through each wave as it moved onward to its eventual destination. I could tell that this ship was on a mission.

While this ship looked like any other ship you would see from that time period, there was something very different about it. On the front sail was the number "412" and on its side was the number "15." While I had no idea what the picture meant, I knew two things: first, this picture was from God, and the second thing I knew was that the number 15 was for me personally. Over the years, the number 15 has been used by God, again and again, to confirm things for me.

I knew this picture that came into my heart at the end of my prayer time was God calling me come deeper to seek an answer from Him on what this meant. I love what Proverbs 25:2 states: *"It is* the glory of God to conceal a matter, But the glory of kings *is* to search out a matter."

While this picture only lasted for a few seconds, it left a deep impression within my spirit. I knew it was meant for me, mainly through the peace I felt and the number 15. However, I had no idea what the number 412 meant. As with any potential revelation, I wrote it in my journal and just made a point to pray over it. If it was from God, He would eventually explain it to me.

GOD BEGINS TO REVEAL
THE PURPOSE OF THE VISION

As with many prophetic words, this one was filed away, but was not forgotten. Over the next few months, I brought it up before the Lord, trying to see if there was anything new to discover from it. I had committed to not trying to force it to match something, but it was crazy how many times I saw 412. We even stayed in a hotel and they moved us to another room, and you guessed it; it was room 412. God was putting 412 in front of my eyes in all kinds of places, but I knew if it was from God, He would eventually reveal the meaning.

It wasn't until April of that next year that I finally discovered the true meaning behind this picture of a ship with 412 on its front sail. I not only discovered the meaning of it, more importantly I understood the direction God was giving me through that picture for praying for our nation. The number 412 became a road sign directing me further into the destiny God has for America.

The discovery came as I was preparing to lead a prayer gathering on The National Day of Prayer in the spring of 2020. As I was researching several significant historical prayer events, ones that helped in the founding of this country as a Christian nation, I discovered one that was very significant.

CAPE HENRY AND THE REV. ROBERT HUNT

In the year of 1607, the Jamestown Expedition landed at the shores of modern-day Cape Henry, Virginia, to establish the first American colony in what would be called Jamestown, named after King James I. When they arrived, they waited offshore for three days, fasting and praying before they set foot on the shoreline. They knew this was significant, so they took their time to be spiritually prepared. Once the landing party was on shore, they planted a cross on the beach that they had brought with them from England, and The Rev. Robert Hunt led them in the following prayer while they planted the cross on the beach.

> We do hereby dedicate this Land, and ourselves, to reach the People within these shores with the Gospel of Jesus Christ, and to raise up Godly generations after us, and with these generations take the Kingdom of God to all the earth. May this Covenant of Dedication remain to all generations, as long as this earth remains, and may this Land, along with England, be Evangelist to the World. May all who see this Cross, remember what we have done here, and may those who come here to inhabit join us in this Covenant and in this most noble work that the Holy Scriptures may be fulfilled.[9]

As I read this powerful prayer while preparing to lead a prayer gathering for the National Day of Prayer, I could feel these powerful words were tied to my growing desire to pray for America. I have always loved history, and despite how many books I have collected, I was never aware of this prayer. As I studied, it became clear this was much more than just a prayer; this sounded like a declaration or decree. Have you ever seen when someone dedicates a building and they cut a ribbon while making a statement dedicating the building for a particular purpose? It was as if the Rev. Robert Hunt was cutting the ribbon on the new land and dedicating it for its purpose.

THE POWER OF A DECREE

In the book of Job, we read about the power of a decree: "You will also declare a thing, And it will be established for you" (Job 22:28). The word decree is defined by the Collins Dictionary as, "an official order or decision, especially one made by the ruler of a country."[10]

I'm not sure if the Rev. Hunt knew what he was really doing when he prayed that prayer, and it really doesn't matter because God knew. God knew we were destined to become a beachhead for the Gospel of His kingdom and that is why Rev. Robert Hunt prayed that prayer. If you doubt that, all you need to do is look at all of the writings of the Founding Fathers of our country. God's fingerprints are all over them.

THE MYSTERY OF 412 IS REVEALED

I did not immediately make the connection between the vision of the ship I had the previous year and this new revelation of what Rev. Hunt did on that shoreline of modern-day Virginia, but I somehow knew the ship with the number 412 on its forward sail was connected. The breakthrough came when I looked up the ship that Robert Hunt sailed on across the Atlantic Ocean. The ship was called the *Susan Constant,* and when I pulled up a picture, I noticed it looked just like the ship in my vision.

Later that week, I felt prompted to look up the date of my vision in relation to the date Robert Hunt made that powerful decree. My vision came on June 11th of 2019. Rev. Hunt made that decree in April of 1607. That makes my vision 412 years after he spoke that prayer and decree. Not to the day, but it still was 412 years later. I was satisfied with that alone as confirmation of what 412 meant, but also felt there was more to discover.

As I researched further, I saw something more specific. I had my vison in June of 2019 after taking communion. The Rev. Robert Hunt led the first settlers in Jamestown in their first communion in the new land the next week of June in 1607.[11] I got chill bumps after I realized it was almost 412 years to the day and I was doing exactly what they were doing.

As I prayed about this revelation, God made it clear that I was to pray He would restore us back to that covenant first established in 1607. This was quite obviously becoming my calling. How did I know for sure? The "streams" I had been drinking from were getting the same message I was, but with even deeper clarity.

One of those streams came from Apostle Dutch Sheets. While I was already familiar with his ministry and his teachings on prayer, God used him to open the floodgates of understanding of the destiny of America. My initial understanding of the significance of Rev. Hunt and Cape Henry was limited, but Dutch opened that up to a whole new level of understanding. God has truly given him a call for America, and his teachings and ministry continue to educate and lead people also called to pray for America.

MY ANCESTORS SPEAK

Shortly after I made the connection between my vision in 2019 and Rev. Robert Hunt's declaration, I made another discovery that led me even deeper into my call to pray for America. I learned my own ancestor William Hancock came to America in 1619 to help establish the next settlement just up the river from Jamestown. This was the second settlement created by King James I for the purpose of colonizing America. The company they formed was called the Berkeley Company, which later led to the establishment of the Berkeley Plantation.

Not long after that I learned that the group William Hancock landed with has been recognized for celebrating the very first Thanksgiving in America. They had sailed from England on the small ship, *Margaret,* and when they arrived on December 4th, 1619, Captain John Woodlief and the Anglican missionary George Thorpe led the other thirty-six men ashore, including my ancestor. They then followed orders they had been given in England: that upon the ship's arrival, the date of landing should be kept yearly as a day of thanksgiving. Today, a plaque is posted at Berkeley Plantation that states, "The first official, annual Thanksgiving in America was observed by Berkeley's brave adventurers on December 4, 1619."[12]

God not only led me to an important spiritual event in America's spiritual history, He also led me to an important spiritual event in my own family history. All of this was through a vision I had praying one day in my home office in 2019. The point is this: God was using a vision to call me to pray for our nation. While you don't have to receive a vision from God to pray for America, you do need to *gain* vision of what God wants for her in order to pray effectively.

WHAT GOD WANTED ME TO KNOW

I believe God wants us to know a few things about America. First, America was birthed with a spiritual purpose from God. God has established America to become a beachhead for His purposes. Beachhead is defined as a "secure initial position that has been gained and can be used for further advancement; foothold."[13] God wants us to hold and protect what has been gained, not for the glory of America, but for the purposes of His kingdom. God also wants us to know we all play an important role in His plans for America. Your vote matters greatly, but your prayers and actions matter even more.

GOD HAS CALLED YOU TO PRAY
FOR REIGN IN AMERICA

Most of us know that God has called us to pray for the destiny of our nation. There are some who teach that we should only focus on the work of the church, but nothing could be further from the truth. Just look at the pattern of God in His Word. "And seek the peace of the city where I have caused you to be carried away captive, and pray to the Lord for it; for in its peace you will have peace" (Jeremiah 29:7).

> God wants us to hold and protect what has been gained, not for the glory of America, but for the purposes of His kingdom.

When the children of Israel were carried off into bondage, God commanded them to pray for the peace of that godless city. Another version uses the word prosperity in place of the word peace. If God commanded His people to pray for the blessing of an evil empire, how much more should we pray for one that has become a blessing and a beachhead for His kingdom purposes?

THE REASON MANY CHRISTIANS FAIL
TO PRAY FOR AMERICA

I know most people will agree with me when I say we need to pray for America, but many fail to do it consistently. I believe the biggest reason this happens is that they simply doubt their prayers are truly making any difference. They watch the news and it seems like things are only getting worse. Too many Christians are hindered from praying for America, not by Satan, but by their own unbelief.

> Too many Christians are hindered from praying for America, not by Satan, but by their own unbelief.

They unfortunately believe their prayers are having little or no effect, but nothing could be further from the truth. Every prayer matters in the kingdom of God.

I can understand the discouragement some feel when praying for our country. It can be difficult to track any measurable results, at least in a short time. It's one thing to pray for a specific person or a personal situation, something where it's small enough that you can actually gauge the effectiveness of your prayers over time. It's another thing to have prayed for almost forty years for an unjust decision to be overturned with little or no results year after year. Just ask any of the seasoned prayer warriors who have prayed for the overturn of *Roe v. Wade,* sending the decision regarding abortion back to the states. If you were to ask one of these "generals of prayer"—men and women like Dutch Sheets and Cindy Jacobs—I'm sure they would share that it was a difficult journey. A difficult journey with many setbacks, but so worth the sacrifice and perseverance that it took.

If you are going to pray for this nation, you need to realize that prayer is not magic, it's war. To effectively pray for America, you cannot obtain your motivation to pray just from the results. Motivation must primarily come from Heaven. If you are results-motivated, you will give out and give up if the war drags on for years. Don't receive only your marching orders from Heaven, receive your encouragement and motivation as well. The victories will come eventually, but your source of strength needs to be consistent if you are going to persevere in prayer.

> **To effectively pray for America, you cannot obtain your motivation to pray just from the results. Motivation must primarily come from Heaven.**

THE PRAYERS OF JUST ONE PERSON

I started this book talking about a man named Rees Howells who prayed for his nation: the nation of Great Britain. God used him to lead others in prayer during the darkest days of WWII, and God answered those prayers, in dramatic fashion.

I am sure Rees battled the thought, "Am I really making a difference?" Especially when some things did not turn out as he had hoped. I believe Rees Howells learned a secret about prevailing prayer that helped him not to rely on the news as his final source when evaluating whether his prayers were effective.

We really never know the full impact of one man or woman's prayers. In the end, it may have been the prayers of Rees Howells and the team he led that actually turned the war around. God may have been giving intelligence reports to them on the movements of the enemy; not so they could pass it on to the leaders of the English military, but so that they would pray and intercede. I personally believe the Miracle of Dunkirk was the work of God, but it was in concert with the prayers of many intercessors like Rees Howells who came into agreement with God through prayer.

YOU MIGHT BE THE NEXT REES HOWELLS

Can you even begin to believe that your prayers have the ability by themselves to impact America? If you have doubted this, I want to challenge you here, because your prayers have the potential to turn America toward God—even if you were the only one praying.

You may be thinking, "How can one man really have that type of impact on a nation?" I would suggest you listen to a famous queen who led Scotland from 1542 until 1567. Mary Stuart—better known as Mary, Queen of Scots—made a very famous and often-quoted statement about a Scottish minister who was a reformed theologian and also the leader of The Scottish Reformation. The Reverend John Knox had incredible influence during his time. He was the founder of the Presbyterian Church of Scotland, but Queen Mary knew him to be a man of prayer. In fact, the potential opposition he brought to her reign was not in his theology, but in his prayers. Of Knox, Queen Mary is reported to have said: "I fear the prayers of John Knox more than all the assembled armies of Europe."[14]

Can one person's prayers have an impact on a nation? Just ask Queen Mary.

The prayer and decree of Rev. Robert Hunt has had powerful influence on the work of God in America. Just look at what has happened over the last two-hundred-plus years when it comes to sending missionaries into the mission field.

The United States has led the way worldwide in sending out missionaries, sending out over 127,000 of the world's estimated 400,000 missionaries abroad.[15] These statistics were reported in 2010 by Todd Johnson, director of the Center for the Study of Global Christianity at Gordon-Conwell Theological Seminary in Massachusetts. America has fulfilled those words Rev. Hunt prayed when he said, "We do hereby dedicate this Land, and ourselves, to reach the People within these shores with the Gospel of Jesus Christ, and to raise up Godly generations after us, and with these generations take the Kingdom of God to all the earth."

> **"I fear the prayers of John Knox more than all the assembled armies of Europe."**
> **Mary, Queen of Scots**

HOW TO PRAY FOR REIGN IN AMERICA

Here are twelve keys to help you effectively Pray for Reign in America.

Ask God to share His heart with you regarding America. As simple as this sounds, it can have profound results. While God does not love America more than He loves any other nation, He does have a specific purpose in mind for her and the people who call her home. Ask Him to share it with you, so that you can not only help carry it, but more importantly, pray for it.

Ask the Holy Spirit to guide you. There is no greater prayer partner than the Holy Spirit. He will not only guide on how to pray; He will empower your prayers as you allow Him to lead you.

Study God's Word. The man or woman who walks in prayer authority is one who understands what their spiritual authority really is. The basis of authority in prayer is the Word of God. Immerse yourself in His Word. Pray God's Word over America as the Spirit leads you.

Don't let the news be your primary source for direction. If you allow the news to direct your prayers, you may find yourself praying reactive prayers rather than Spirit-led prayers. This does not mean God will not use a news report to draw your attention to something, but don't let it become your primary source for how you pray. Interpret the news by the Word, not vice versa.

Don't be pulled into a political spirit. There is a big difference between praying for a political candidate because you believe God has directed you to pray for them versus praying for someone because they are in a political party you prefer. When praying for America, let God be your guide; not just the voting list of the party you are registered with.

Remember the goal. The end goal is not just to have a prosperous America where everyone's dreams come true. The end goal of Praying for Reign in America is partnering and agreeing with God through prayer for the fulfillment of His plan—His plan to manifest His kingdom realm in America as it is in Heaven. In other words, it's to continue the plans and purposes of God for our nation; the ones that were decreed by Rev. Robert Hunt over four hundred years ago. While we want America to prosper and enjoy the favor of God, it's not the primary goal.

Take Prayer Journeys. I will go into more detail about this later in the book, but God will use these journeys and assignments to deepen your calling to pray for America and also to provide you with spiritual intel. Once you have stood before the Supreme Court building and prayed for a godly decision, your prayers will never be the same again.

Make a prayer board. This can be as elaborate as turning your whole study or home office into a prayer room, or it can be as simple as having a charm bracelet with charms representing things you specifically pray for regarding America. I have a souvenir key ring with the words "White House Oval Office" written on it. I often hold it when I am praying for the White House or the President.

Study History. Just as the story of Rev. Robert Hunt's prayer opened my eyes to America's spiritual history, there are many historical accounts to be discovered from our nation. Buried within America's history is the story of God's plan to establish liberty for the purposes of His kingdom.

Connect with ministries that pray for our nation. There are many ministries that have dedicated themselves to praying for America. Connecting to them will not only provide you with leadership and direction, it will also become a great source of encouragement. I personally have loved drinking from the stream of the ministries of Dutch Sheets and Ken Malone. These apostolic leaders of prayer carry a special mantle for leading and equipping many in the Body of Christ for prayer.

Persevere in Prayer. While I would love to tell you that praying for America and the purposes of God for her is easy, that would not be telling you the truth. Great victories in prayer come through those who have not only heard God but are willing to kneel until the answer comes. This is why our motivation and encouragement must come from the throne of God, and not just the mouths of men.

Pass it on to the next generation. While it is vital that we play our part in Praying for Reign for America, it is absolutely essential that we pass it on to the next generation. If we don't, then when our lives end, the prayers may end as well. Take time to pray with your kids or grandkids for America. Prayer is more often caught than taught. They will learn more on prayer journeys with their grandparents than they ever will sitting in a Sunday school class. While it's important we pray, we cannot fail in raising up the next generation to do likewise. Who knows, it might be your grandson or granddaughter that becomes the next Rees Howells or John Knox?

SECTION THREE

LORD, TEACH US TO PRAY

Learning How to Pray for Reign

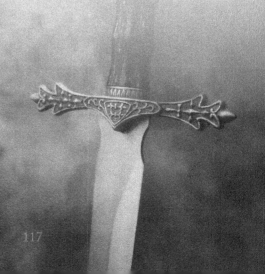

Chapter Nine

THE MODEL PRAYER

Praying for Reign Through the Lord's Prayer

I f you had the chance to personally learn from someone living now or from the past on the subject of prayer, who would that be and why? Just imagine if you could get not just a quick afternoon, but ongoing training on how to pray like they did. Who would you pick? At the top of my list are a few people who immediately come to mind.

Count Zinzendorf. I would want to learn from him because God used him to lead a nomadic community called the Moravians into a lifestyle of prayer that was twenty-four hours a day, and lasted for over one hundred years.

Rees Howells. It would take a week or two just to listen to the stories from this prayer giant. No one understood and lived intercession like Rees Howells did. Stories from his life are listed all throughout this book, since he is one of greatest examples of how a true leader of prayer can transform the world through the power of prayer and intercession.

While these and many more names on my list are powerful, there is one that is above them all. If I could only pick one to learn from there is no doubt that I would call on the greatest intercessor of all time, the Lord Jesus Christ. He is not only the greatest instructor of prayer for you and me, He was also the greatest instructor for His disciples. They wanted Him to teach them to pray. They wanted Him to teach them because of the things they saw Him do.

THE DISCIPLES SAW A LOT

The disciples and followers of Jesus saw a lot. They observed His teachings which confounded even the wisest scholars of that day. They also watched Him perform miracles no one had ever seen before. They were firsthand witnesses to amazing works of power mixed with compassion as He healed many. No one had ever had this type of power.

Can you imagine if you were one of the disciples and had a front-row seat to everything Jesus did? What would you have asked Jesus to teach you to do?

- Would you have asked Him how to teach you how to turn water into wine?
- Would you have asked Him to teach you how to multiply food and feed thousands with only enough food for one or two people?
- Would you have asked Him to teach you how to have power over demons or the elements?

What is amazing to many who have read through The Gospels is that there is never a time recorded when the disciples asked Jesus to teach them any of those things. The only request for personal instruction was when one of His disciples asked Jesus to teach him and the other disciples how to pray.

> One day, as Jesus was in prayer, one of his disciples came over to him as he finished and said, "Would you teach us a model prayer that we can pray, just as John did for his disciples?" Luke 11:1 (TPT)

What did the disciples see?

- They saw Jesus come out of times of prayer with the power to heal any and every disease.
- They saw Jesus come back from times of secret prayer, sometimes all night long, with an authority that caused demons to flee.
- They saw the rhythm and cycle of His life: from prayer to power to prayer again.

THE EXAMPLE OF POPEYE THE SAILOR

A great example of this would be from the classic cartoon, *Popeye the Sailor*. When I was a small boy, I would sit for hours on end watching all of my favorite cartoons throughout the week. I loved Popeye. The more I watched the cartoon, the more I wanted to eat spinach. I think my mother put me in front of the television on purpose because it became apparent to me that every time Popeye ate spinach, he gained superhuman strength. It always seemed that he ate it just at the right time, just when his strength was tapped out.

> **If Jesus—who was fully God and fully man—needed to pray, then how much more do we need to pray?**

Seeing was believing, so I believed that spinach would make me strong enough to run over all the neighborhood kids in a game of tackle football.

While Jesus was not opening a can of spinach to gain all His strength, He was in a sense opening up the door to Heaven through prayer. The disciples saw Him do this over and over again. As I look at the life of Jesus, I have to ask myself, "If Jesus—who was fully God and fully man—needed to pray, then how much more do we need to pray?"

LORD, TEACH US TO PRAY

A particular disciple came to Jesus in Luke 11. He came because he saw something. Something that Jesus was doing that he and his partners in faith needed to know. They needed to know how to pray like Jesus.

There are many teachings from Jesus on prayer, but none like the one He gave to His disciples after the request to teach them how to pray. Some call it the "Lord's Prayer" while many others call it the "Disciples' Prayer," since it was for the disciples. It is recorded in two gospels, Luke and Matthew. So what is it that makes this prayer so powerful?

Before I answer that question, my question for you to consider is this: Have you ever thought deeply about The Lord's Prayer? Or, like many others, have you just recounted it without thinking about what Jesus was teaching through it?

I love the scene in the movie *Woodlawn* where the coaches and the sports chaplain are leading the stadium in The Lord's Prayer. In the movie, based on a true story, a school administrator who wants to shut down all spiritual meetings on campus unplugs the PA system they are using to lead everyone in the prayer. As the trio can no longer be heard, the thousands who are attending this game can be heard finishing the rest of this ancient but powerful prayer. What a powerful scene.

> **Have you ever thought deeply about The Lord's Prayer? Or, like many others, have you just recounted it without thinking about what Jesus was teaching through it?**

It seems to me that this prayer has always been tied to sports. For as long as I can remember, I prayed this before and after football games, both as a coach and as a player. While it had incredible power and purpose exactly as we recited it, it was meant for so much more. Inside this prayer is an outline for how all prayer should be done. Inside this special prose of spiritual power is a code—a code that will open all of us up to a deeper and more meaningful relationship with God.

GOD GAVE US A GIFT

Within the Lord's Prayer we are given what I like to call the "Kingdom Prayer Code." It's a gift that can't be fully taught in one sitting, because it continues to teach us more and more as we grow in Christ and are led by the Holy Spirit. This prayer is actually a door that leads not just into prayer, but more importantly into a lifestyle of prayer. Most of all, the Lord's Prayer leads us to the Father, who is both the answer and the source of all of our prayers.

THE LORD'S PRAYER IS REALLY AN OUTLINE

Before we begin, it's important to understand that The Lord's Prayer is really a prayer outline. Many who teach on prayer have shared the following concept: Jewish teachers of that day would often teach their students by giving them an outline or a parable. The beginning outline was a way to impart to them the basis of the teaching. Students would then follow up that outline with more information that would essentially fill in the blanks or complete the teaching. Even when you look at other teachings of Jesus, you can observe times when He started with a parable and then would follow up with a full explanation of what it really meant.

> Most of all, the Lord's Prayer leads us to the Father, who is both the answer and the source of all of our prayers.

So if it is an outline, then it needs to be explained deeper, but we never read in scripture where Jesus went on to fully explain the prayer beyond what was taught. If we are to truly understand all that it means, then how is that done? Who will teach us or fill in the blanks? This is done by both the Word of God and the Holy Spirit.

Yes, you can gain great value just out of the basic truths that are in this powerful prayer, but to fully understand it we need someone to explain it to us; someone who knows what Jesus was teaching us. I love what George Mueller stated about the work of the Holy Spirit when it came to explaining the Word of God:

"God then began to show me that the Word of God alone is our standard of judgment in spiritual things; that it can be explained only by the Holy Spirit; and that in our day, as well as in former times, He is the teacher of His people."

THE LORD'S PRAYER IS A POWERFUL KINGDOM-BUILDING PRAYER

At the heart of the Lord's Prayer is a powerful outline; one that is designed to empower His followers in fulfilling the Great Commission. While I am so thankful God will hear the prayer of any one person who is willing to turn to Him for help, this prayer had a power strategy attached to it. This prayer is not just a prayer to pray on special occasions; this is a prayer that opens up Heaven.

> This is not just a prayer to pray on special occasions; this a prayer that opens up Heaven.

BREAKING DOWN THE OUTLINE OF THE LORD'S PRAYER

Below is a breakdown of the prayer and what I've learned as I have asked the Holy Spirit to lead and guide me. Seeking the Holy Spirit's guidance through scripture can take a while as you weigh what you have read with what you are hearing or sensing. The Holy Spirit loves to take you throughout the Word of God, utilizing the whole counsel of God to speak to and direct you. What I've heard as I have asked Him to unpack this outline for me is nothing strange, but rather a powerful, yet personal, expansion of the prayer. The Holy Spirit is not changing it, but unpacking it and expanding it so that it becomes a personal way of praying. He is filling in the blanks of the outline and He will do the same for you if you ask Him.

Now it came to pass, as He was praying in a certain place, when He ceased, that one of His disciples said to Him, "Lord, teach us to pray, as John also taught his disciples." Luke 11:1

While this request with the subsequent prayer is recorded in the Gospel of Luke, I am using the version that is found in the Gospel of Matthew to teach more about each element of the prayer.

> In this manner, therefore, pray:
> Our Father in heaven,
> Hallowed be Your name.
> Your kingdom come.
> Your will be done
> On earth as it is in heaven.
> Give us this day our daily bread.
> And forgive us our debts,
> As we forgive our debtors.
> And do not lead us into temptation,
> But deliver us from the evil one.
> For Yours is the kingdom and the power and the glory
> forever. Amen. Matthew 6:9-13

OUR FATHER IN HEAVEN: IT ALL BEGINS WITH THE FATHER

"Our Father in Heaven" (Matthew 6:9)

In the Passion Translation it says "our Heavenly Father." The Aramaic word used here by Jesus is "Abba." Jesus begins with this statement because this entire prayer is built upon this revelation and understanding that God is our Heavenly Father, our Abba. Abba is one of the most intimate terms that when spoken in Aramaic; it expresses intimacy with God as our Father. Some would say that using this word is like someone saying "Daddy" or "Papa."

When praying the Lord's Prayer, it must begin with the reality of who God really is as our Heavenly Father. God wants us to know that He is not just an unknown creator who rules from a hidden place somewhere within our universe. No, God is our Abba and while He fills the whole universe, He also wants to fill our lives and hearts as well.

One of the most unfortunate stumbling blocks for modern Christians is that so many Christians carry the heartache of not having had a good father in their life. Nothing inhibits our ability to see and know God as He really is, our Heavenly Father, like having an earthly dad who was not a good example of a loving father. While no father is perfect—even the best dads come short of who Father God is—there are some who lived so far below that standard that it is very hard to see God through the frame they created.

The good news is God can change all of that; in fact, He wants to change that right now. He not only wants to heal you, He also wants to help you forgive him. Many times, people who have experienced the "father wound" of not having a good father carry hidden unforgiveness toward God Himself. They think, "Why couldn't God have stepped in and helped my father be a good father? Why didn't He help me?"

The trauma of those wounds is all very real to the person who struggles with them. While great teachers and counselors can help lead someone to understand how to forgive their father and even God, no one can help you through this like the Holy Spirit can. Even if you choose to get counseling to get over a father-wound, ask the Holy Spirit to help you. For this reason, the first part of the Lord's Prayer is also a place of healing. Healing that enables one to really pray in kingdom power.

To be able to pray the Lord's Prayer in power, it must begin with a true belief that God is your Heavenly Father. That you are a son or a daughter of the King of the universe. It can't be just an opening statement of respect; it must become a reality.

Why is it so important to have this very first point established if we are going to pray the Lord's Prayer in power? It is important because this prayer cannot take off without us knowing Him not just as God, but also as our Father. If we don't learn to know Him as our Father, then we will not recognize His power at work in our lives. And if we do not recognize His power at work in our lives, we will ultimately rely upon our own. True dependance begins with recognizing the source of our dependence.

> If we don't learn to know Him as our Father, then we will not recognize His power at work in our lives. And if we do not recognize His power at work in our lives, we will ultimately rely upon our own.

HALLOWED BE YOUR NAME: KNOWING WHO WE ARE BEGINS WITH KNOWING WHO HE REALLY IS.

"Hallowed be Your name." (Matthew 6:9)

I love how the Passion Translation states it: "May the glory of your name be the center on which our life turns" (Luke 11:2).

When you hear the name of God, what do you think? Way down inside, what do you really feel? Does it move you? Does it excite you and build your faith, or is it just a name you have used when you want to talk about the creator or the "Big Man."

Throughout scripture there are several names that are used to refer to God. All of them carry great power as they work to paint a picture of who God really is. What is amazing is that God is so great, so immeasurable, that no English or even Hebrew names can fully describe all that He really is. He is truly beyond our full comprehension, but desires to reveal Himself to us.

HOLY, HOLY, HOLY

I have heard this illustration for years. It is built around the scripture in Revelation where the angels in Heaven are saying "Holy, Holy, Holy," over and over again. To us who live in the natural realm of earth it is easy to think, "How in the world can that continue over and over again for eternity?" We know that God is great, but I have often thought, "How long can they keep saying that without it becoming rote?"

The illustration I remember hearing is of God turning Himself and showing a new side of His glory to the angels, almost like a multi-faceted diamond being turned to show another glimpse of its shimmer. Imagine if God is like a diamond, not with hundreds of different facets but with trillions or even unlimited. This illustration continues as God shows another part of His nature or His glory, and each time He does it is so thrilling to the angels that they spin around and bow down, saying, "Holy, Holy, Holy," all over again. I like to picture God saying, "Here is a new one you haven't seen before." And once again they are moved to worship. Endless facets, endless beauty, endless power, endless Glory.

While we are not able to see whatever the angels in Heaven are seeing, incredibly we are the temple of God. For God Himself lives in our heart if we have been born again. He dwells in us, but what's going to move us into His very presence is how we view Him. If we hold Him and His name in a high esteem then we will enter His holy presence, with our own hearts spinning and twirling around the glory of His name.

> "May the glory of your name be the center on which our lives turn" (Matthew 6:9 TPT).

A NAME CAN TELL YOU A LOT ABOUT A PERSON

I love researching my family history. I could spend days on Ancestory.com; I am not a paid spokesperson for them, but I might as well be because I love what they do. It's so cool putting in the names you know and watching those green leaves light up, leading you to the next generation.

I have found through my extensive late-night research that I have many ancestors and family lines that had significance in not only this country, but also in Great Britain. I have discovered I am related to the Spencer family, which makes me the twenty-second cousin of Prince William and Prince Harry. I don't expect to be invited for tea anytime soon, but it's pretty cool to be related to the royal family, Winston Churchill, and the late Lady Diana.

I am also related to several Founding Fathers of this nation. The Hancocks, including John Hancock who signed the Declaration of Independence and William Hancock who came to America in the second wave of settlements from England, are relatives of mine. Valentine Hollingsworth, who was part of establishing Pennsylvania with William Penn, is my great-great-grandfather.

I literally could go on and on because it not only excites me to search out the names of my ancestors, but it also thrills me to share them with others. Their stories not only tell the tale of who they were, they also tell the story of who I am. Just as their names bring their stories to life, the names used throughout scripture to describe God are not just the names of a distant God; these are the names of our Father. In essence these names are our own unique faith-based family tree. Just look at some of the names of God that are used throughout the Old Testament:

Jehovah Jireh (The Lord Will Provide)
Jehovah Mekoddishkem (The Lord Who Sanctifies You)
Jehovah Nissi (The Lord My Banner)
Jehovah-Raah (The Lord My Shepherd)
Jehovah Rapha (The Lord That Heals)
Jehovah Sabaoth (The Lord of Hosts)
Jehovah Shammah (The Lord Is There)
Jehovah Shalom (The Lord Is Peace)

Jehovah Tsidkenu (The Lord Our Righteousness)
El Shaddai (Lord God Almighty)
El Elyon (The Most High God)
Adonai (Lord, Master)
Yahweh (Lord, Jehovah)
El Olam (The Everlasting God)
Elohim (God)
Qanna (Jealous)

Thank God He has given us His names. As His heirs we have been given His kingdom, and while we will never be God, we are His children and joint heirs with His son. As you pray through this portion of the Lord's Prayer, ask the Holy Spirit to reveal the power of God's names to you.

YOUR KINGDOM COME: THE COMMAND FOR PRAYING FOR REIGN

"Your kingdom come. Your will be done
On earth as it is in heaven" (Matthew 6:10)

This is a one of the most powerful requests we could ever make as a child of God on earth. Just look at it in its full line: "Your kingdom come, Your will be done, On earth as it is in heaven."

As the first request of the Lord's Prayer, this prayer is calling for the reign of God to come to earth, just as it is in Heaven. I do not know if you realize it or not, but we are incredibly blessed to even be able to ask this of our Creator. Never, ever take this for granted because these three lines contain the power of God to build and extend His kingdom through us, His church. If you ever doubt that you, along with the Apostle Peter, have been given the keys of the kingdom of Heaven then you need to take a good look at this first request.

I love how the Passion Translation puts it: "Manifest your kingdom realm, and cause your every purpose to be fulfilled on earth, just as it is in heaven" (Matthew 6:10).

As I shared earlier in this book, God does not need our permission, but He does seek and require our agreement. This is how our Sovereign God has set it up.

THY KINGDOM COME: LET THE INVASION BEGIN

One of the best illustrations of what this means to me can be found in combat, especially during an invasion like D-Day. In that scenario, you would have a soldier on the ground who has a radio, one of the most important tools for any battle. As in the case of an invasion, he may be calling in air support or requesting instructions on what comes next. This is a great picture of who we really are in prayer. We are on the ground, invading darkness with light. As we use our radio of prayer, we are calling for the release of God's plans and purposes on earth. Imagine that headquarters is where God is situated, and just like a military general who is planning and overseeing the advance of his army, God has His own map room. In this map room, our Commander can see what He has planned out. Even though we cannot see the entire plan, we can depend on Him not only to direct us to our objective, but to move us around the trenches and landmines of the enemy.

The general has plans that will lead to victory, and unlike the foot soldier, he can see things they cannot see. In God's divine providence, He has decided to work with us, relying on us to ask not only for support but also so His plans and purposes can be released. More than just asking for them, He also needs us to be part of implementing and deploying them. "Your kingdom come" is not just asking God to invade the world and take it over. That is what the disciples hoped as well. Praying "your kingdom come" is to ask God to:

1. Do things only He can do. (There are things He can do from headquarters.)
2. Direct us.
3. Empower us.
4. Provide for us.
5. Protect us.

When we pray this part of the prayer, we are basically saying, "God, put your plan into motion and show me what part I am to play in it." Praying "your kingdom come" is asking God to launch His invasion and assign you to your mission.

I believe Jesus taught His disciples this prayer because this is how He prayed. I can imagine Jesus praying this prayer, asking for the kingdom of God to move into the earth, and then He is directed to go through Samaria because the next campaign of the kingdom was for the village of Sycar. When we understand that Jesus is the one on earth with the earthly authority to call for it, then we can understand the authority we have been given in prayer. The late Dr. Myles Monroe said it best: "Prayer is man giving God permission or license to interfere in earth's affairs."

> **Praying "your kingdom come" is asking God to launch His invasion and assign you to your mission.**

As Jesus was giving Peter the keys to the kingdom, He was giving him not only the radio to communicate with headquarters, but also the authority to call for whatever was necessary for a successful campaign. It's powerful to see how God will use us to call for the kingdom of God to come into the earth, that what has been planned out and established in Heaven would also be done on earth.

As you pray this part it is important that you pray for the power of His kingdom to come:

- In your life.
- In your family.

- In your community.
- On your job.
- In your state.
- In your nation.

As you ask for His kingdom to come, you are also asking for Him to give you:

- Your assignment.
- The direction you will need.
- The authority you will require.
- The power to accomplish and fulfill your assignment.

GIVE US OUR DAILY BREAD: OUR ALLEGIANCE TO DEPEND ON GOD

"Give us this day our daily bread" (Matthew 6:11)

I have asked for God to bring His kingdom realm into the earth and to use me as part of that, but now I need His ongoing provision. What is amazing is that God already knows what I need before I ask, and encourages me not to worry about it. Then why are we being taught to ask for everything we need, our daily bread? This part of the prayer is not begging God for provision, it is recognizing that He is our provider. To pray this is to clearly say that I am dependent on God for everything I need. It's kind of a pledge of sorts, one that pledges our allegiance to God as our sole provider.

Is it scary to you to be fully dependent on God for everything? While I hope this will help make you feel better, the truth is you already are fully dependent on God. If He didn't bring the rain, we would either die of hunger or thirst. If the sun was to shift one direction or the other, we could either freeze or burn up. No matter what you may think, we are all fully dependent on God. The question is not if are we dependent on God, the question is do we recognize and exercise our dependency through active trust and faith?

GEORGE MUELLER: A LESSON OF DEPENDENCE FOR DAILY BREAD

George Mueller understood the principle of relying on God for daily bread very well. His life and ministry demonstrated a true recognition of dependence on God for everything. As a pastor in Bristol, England in the early 1800's, he became concerned by many of the orphans who seemed to be everywhere.[16] This concern led him to open an orphanage, but God had given him direction to do it without any dependence on man or by means of fundraising. If George needed something like food or money to pay the bills, he would go to God for it, not man. He saw this as an opportunity to not only help the orphans, but to also demonstrate to people that they can depend on God for everything they needed.

As George continued to follow God in his ministry, he continued to build more orphanages, depending totally on God for the resources he needed. He would ask God to provide everything from the building to the very people who would help to run it.

One of my favorite stories about the ministry of George Mueller paints a clear picture of his dependence on God, and it played out in front of him and the many children he and his staff cared for. As it is recorded in Mueller's journals, Mueller was informed one morning that the children were dressed and ready for school but there was no food for them to eat. One can only imagine the overwhelming concern from having an orphanage with hundreds of children to only discover you have no food to feed them.

George asked to have the children go into the dining room, where he prayed and thanked God for the food. You are probably asking,

"What food?!" Well, this is one of the secrets of true dependence on God. True dependence on God is expressed most often through thankfulness.

It was not long until George Mueller saw God do what He'd always done: provide what he needed. A knock came to the door and a local baker showed up with fresh bread he'd baked for the orphanage. He told Mueller he was unable to fall asleep so he decided to bake some bread for the children. Not long after the baker arrived, the milkman knocked on the door. His milk cart had broken down and he was afraid the milk would spoil, so he offered it to George for free. All the children were fed that morning, fed through the prayers of one man who knew how to depend on God for daily bread.

FORGIVENESS:
THE KEY TO NOT BEING LEFT BEHIND

"And forgive us our debts,
As we forgive our debtors" (Matthew 6:12)

There is no greater principle in scripture than the principle of forgiving others. This is truly one of the greatest cause-and-effect principles in the Word of God. Just as sowing and reaping is a spiritual law, so is forgiving others and being forgiven. If we were to use the analogy of the combat soldier who is part of an invasion, this would be like saying "Don't pick up an unexploded grenade." The enemy knows the laws of the kingdom, and he knows if he can lead a follower of Christ to become offended, he has a good chance of defeating that soldier.

When we do not know God, when we are lost, He is not our Father but our Judge. That all changes when we are born again. God is no longer seen as our Judge; He now is our Heavenly Father. In Matthew 6:14-15 (TPT), it states:

"And when you pray, make sure you forgive the faults of others so that your Father in heaven will also forgive you.

But if you withhold forgiveness from others, your Father withholds forgiveness from you."

While some think this scripture means that anytime a Christian fails to forgive they have lost their salvation, it really leans toward a much different meaning. If it is true that God becomes our Father once we are born again, then the results of Him withholding forgiveness from His children much more mirrors the discipline of a Father than the judgement of a judge.

This is not to say that unforgiveness is not very serious and totally destructive if held onto. Using the picture of the invading soldier again, if he picks up an unexploded grenade, he is not only going to lose a limb, but he may also lose his life. I truly believe Jesus was saying to His disciples, "If you want to keep following after me, if you want to keep moving forward, then you will have to forgive others along the way." In other words: "Don't pick up any unexploded grenades." Unforgiveness will not only keep you from building the kingdom of God on earth, it will also keep you from building a life.

DELIVER US FROM THE EVIL ONE
RESCUE US FROM THE HAND OF OUR ENEMY

"And do not lead us into temptation,
But deliver us from the evil one." (Matthew 6:13)

We know God is never the author of temptation nor would He lead us into it, but this powerful ending to the Lord's prayer is a recognition that God is our ultimate protector. He is not only our protector; He also is our Deliverer and Rescuer. In Matthew 6:13 (the Passion Translation) it states: "Rescue us every time we face tribulation and set us free from evil. For you are the King who rules with power and glory forever. Amen."

This part is asking for divine guidance. A divine guidance that will lead one through the valley of the shadow of death. Like the daily bread, it's not someone asking God and hoping they'll get an answer, but someone who is sure God promised not only to provide for us, but also to protect us.

Daniel is a living example of one who could boldly live with the understanding that God would protect him until his assignment was complete. He not only saw God protect Shadrach, Meshach, and Abednego through the fiery furnace, but he himself was protected when he was placed into a den of lions.

People have asked me, "If God protected people like Daniel, why didn't He protect the apostles and early Christians who were martyred?" God did protect them: He protected them until their assignment was finished, just as He did with Jesus. A great example of this is found in Acts chapter twelve. In this story, Herod had arrested the Apostle Peter and thrown him in jail. Peter was not just locked in jail; he was also chained up by two chains held between two soldiers. The church prayed, and miraculously an angel came into the jail and released Peter, leading him to safety.

Peter and Daniel were rescued because God was not finished with either one of them. For both of these men, God fulfilled His promise within the Lord's Prayer.

Claiming this promise is to believe that God can deliver us through and from any plan of evil. While we live in a fallen world, one where we can be sure of very little, we can be sure God will be with us through anything. While no life is fully exempt from the pains of tragedy while on this planet, we do know that as His children we have someone who can help us—help us just as He helped Daniel and Peter.

PRAYING THE LORD'S PRAYER

I would greatly encourage you to read through this powerful prayer and ask the Holy Spirit to speak to you through it. While I have shared what the Lord has shown me as I have prayed through it, my goal was not to inform you as much as inspire you. Inspire you to pray the Lord's Prayer and discover how this powerful prayer is the key to both learning how to pray, and learning how to Pray for Reign.

Chapter Ten

THE CROWN, THE KEYS, AND THE SWORD

Understanding the Tools God Has Given You to Pray for Reign.

Not only did Jesus teach His disciples to pray, He also equipped them to pray by giving them the tools and gifts necessary to be effective in prayer. I like to call them gifts, as they are more special than just a tool, but I will refer to them as a tool here so you can understand how they are used. Praying for Reign requires us not only to understand them, but also employ them.

Did you realize Christ has given you everything you need to pray with *power*? The reason I wrote this book was to help Christians truly grasp the power and authority they have in prayer, and to never underestimate it. When properly understood and applied, there is nothing God can't do through a praying Christian. To understand these tools, I want to share something

> **Did you realize Christ has given you everything you need to pray with *power*?**

from my own life to illustrate the importance of receiving the correct tools when it comes to performing your assignment correctly.

AUTHORITY ILLUSTRATED

In 1987, I made a career change in my life by going from a football coach to becoming a state trooper. Being a state trooper was a childhood dream of mine, but it resurfaced again when I was a very young twenty-year-old, newly-married father.

Joining the Florida Highway Patrol was not an easy thing to do. Back then it seemed everyone wanted to be a state trooper so it took a long time to get hired. I was blessed by God to get hired the first year that I applied. Once I was hired, I went through the necessary training and was given my choice of stations. I could be assigned to work out of Miami or Orlando. There was no hesitation for this "North Florida boy," I was taking Orlando.

Before we departed for our station of assignment, we were given items we would need to fulfill our constitutional duties as a state law enforcement officer. I call these items tools because with them I could do my job effectively; without them it would be impossible. The same is true for prayer. As Christians we have been given tools that enable us to pray.

> It's not enough to just understand the tools you have been given to pray; you have to learn how to employ them.

As a state trooper, I was trained not just to understand the tools I'd been given, but in most cases I was trained how to use them very well. It's not enough to just understand the tools you have been given to pray; you have to learn how to employ them.

There were many basic tools necessary for a state trooper—such as a radar to record the speed of vehicles, and handcuffs to make arrests with—but there were three absolutely essential tools I called "The Big Three."

My position: My position as a state trooper was granted to me by the Florida Highway Patrol and the Department of Highway Safety and Motor Vehicles. I just did not decide to make myself a state trooper one afternoon; I had to be selected or chosen. Going through an arduous training at the FHP Training Academy helped me to understand that you were uncommon if you successfully became a state trooper. For the vast majority of state troopers, the powerful understanding that you had been chosen for this role produced a great sense of confidence. There was never any reason to use my power and authority outside of serving and protecting the citizens and visitors of the State of Florida.

My badge: My badge represented more than just a fancy decoration to dress up my uniform. It also established my authority as a state trooper—my authority to investigate accidents, make arrests, and enforce the laws of the state, which was granted to me through the statutes of the State of Florida. I was given legal and statutory authority to perform my duties and my badge backed that authority up. While my confidence rested in the position I'd been given, the charge I had been given to fulfill my duties was totally dependent on the authority that badge held.

My weapons: My weapons were assigned to me by the Florida Highway Patrol and I was fully trained on how to use them. They not only included a handgun and a shotgun, but also other items such as pepper spray and a pr-24 baton. All of these items required certification from an authorized instructor with periodic recertification. While you prayed you never had to use them, you had to be proficient utilizing these tools or they were of no use.

THE BIG THREE OF PRAYER

For the Christian, we also have been given all kinds of tools in order to accomplish our calling to be an effective follower of Christ. Thankfully God has given us everything we need; everything from His Word to the practical spiritual disciplines that enables us to become like Christ. We are fully equipped. To understand how to pray with power, we will need to focus on three elements of those tools. I like to call these the "Big Three of Prayer." If we are going to learn how to Pray for Reign, we will need to understand the meaning behind the crown, the keys, and the sword.

THE CROWN: OUR POSITION IN CHRIST

Before reading this book, did you really know who you are in Christ? Have you been taught that we who believe are joint heirs with Him? As I said earlier, unfortunately many believers struggle with believing they are positionally seated with Christ.

I have counseled many believers who seem to think they are not much different than they were before they were saved. Few seem to understand we are not only different, but our position is different as well. We've already discussed how salvation means that they have both a new final destination called Heaven, and also a new and exciting identity in Christ. The greatest gift that has ever been given to us secures Heaven and a victorious life in the here and now.

There are five crowns found in scripture that will eventually be awarded to believers. The crowns I'm talking about here are not physical crowns, but an understanding of who we really are in Christ. I love the show on Netflix called *The Crown*. In this very popular series, a statement is often uttered by the royal family: "The Crown must take precedence." In our lives as Christians, the crown (or the understanding of who we are) must take precedence as well. For God, who so wonderfully has saved us from darkness, has also translated us into the kingdom. A kingdom where we will serve Him forever as both priests and kings unto our God. As the Bible says, "You have chosen us to serve our God and formed us into a kingdom of priests who reign on the earth" (Revelation 5:10 TPT).

Earlier in Chapter Four, I shared how prayer is the bridge that enables us to know who we really are in Christ, to avoid mistaken identity. Nothing can

> You are not just a sinner who has been saved from hell; you're a sinner who has been translated into a new nature with a brand-new identity and purpose.

be more important than this statement. You are not just a sinner who has been saved from hell; you're a sinner who has been translated into a new nature with a brand-new identity and purpose.

SEEING OUR NEW POSITIONS IN CHRIST

As part of our new identity, God has given us pictures in His word of these new realities. Pictures of what God has made us to be through the miracle known as "new birth." All of these come by way of God's grace, disposed to us His children. We are now:

A New Creation: "Therefore, if anyone is in Christ, he is a new creation; old things have passed away; behold, all things have become new," (2 Corinthians 5:17).

Seated with Christ: "But God, who is rich in mercy, because of His great love with which He loved us, even when we were dead in trespasses, made us alive together with Christ (by grace you have been saved), and raised us up together, and made us sit together in the heavenly places in Christ Jesus, that in the ages to come He might show the exceeding riches of His grace in His kindness toward us in Christ Jesus," (Ephesians 2:4-7).

Joint Heirs with Christ: "For as many as are led by the Spirit of God, these are sons of God. For you did not receive the spirit of bondage again to fear, but you received the Spirit of adoption by whom we cry out, "Abba, Father." The Spirit Himself bears witness with our spirit that we are children of God, and if children, then heirs—heirs of God and joint heirs with Christ, if indeed we suffer with Him, that we may also be glorified together," (Romans 8:14-17).

Even though we are joint-heirs-in-training, we still are joint heirs—and the crown represents not just future rewards we will receive, but it also represents the current reality of who we really are in Christ right now.

His Legal Authority on Earth: Another wonderful thing about our position is that we are an extension of His government here on earth. While there are five crowns that will be awarded to those who believe, there is a positional crown that is worn through an understanding of who we really are as His children and as His "ekklesia."

This might be a new term for some. When Jesus spoke to Peter about building His church in Matthew 16, He used the word "ekklesia" or "ekklesian." That word has been translated in most every version of the Bible to be the word "church," but its original meaning is interesting.

Originally this Greek word was used to describe a Greek assembly, one that would basically create laws and government. This term continued forward as the Romans used it in the same way, but more for regions they had conquered and wanted to make more like Rome. That means that there would have been ekklesia's all over the world where Rome was taking territory and changing culture. In short, this term denotes leadership and governance for those who were placed into that position. As Christ's joint heirs we have been given this position in Him. We are His representatives on earth. I like how the Passion Translation puts this verse:

> I give you the name Peter, a stone. And this rock will
> be the bedrock foundation on which I will build my
> church—my legislative assembly, and the power of death
> will not be able to overpower it! (Matthew 16:18 TPT).

Before we can understand our authority, we must understand our position in Christ. This positional crown is on our head not because of what we did but because of what He did. We are His ekklesia and joint heirs because we are connected by blood to the King, Christ Jesus. When we understand and believe who we really are in Christ, we wear this crown just as a prince or princess would wear one. We have the mind of Christ in what to do, what to pray, and what to decree.

The original word for crown in Greek is "stephanos," and in its meaning it's referred to as a badge of royalty. It can also refer to a prize given in public games when someone was being recognized as the victor or winner of a contest.

While we do not walk around with crowns on our head, make no mistake about it, if you are a follower of Christ then you are no longer just a human being struggling through life, you are now considered royalty.

> Now to the one who *constantly* loves us and has loosed us from our sins by his own blood, and *to the one who* has appointed us as a kingdom of priests to serve his God and Father—to him be glory and dominion throughout the eternity of eternities! Amen! (Revelation 1:5-6 TPT).

Did you read that? We have been appointed as a kingdom of priests (or as some other versions describe it, as kings and priests). I once was given a picture from God about my own new birth experience. This picture He gave me was that of a castle, one that represented Heaven. As I looked at this majestic place through the eyes of my heart, I heard in my spirit a round of trumpeters playing a beautiful fanfare, as if an announcement was coming. As this picture continued in my heart, I heard within me a loud voice announce the birth of a new son into the royal family. The voice said, "Donald Lane Newman was born into the royal family on this day." As the announcement was made, there was loud applause everywhere. While this was only a picture, it painted a true reality. When we are born again, we don't just escape hell, we enter the royal family. I was literally overwhelmed by this, knowing that being born again means we are no longer the same person.

There is nothing the devil fights more than our newfound identity in Christ. He will tell every lie to discount and destroy the truth that we are Christ's joint heirs and co-regents. The enemy will use anything at his disposal to convince us to take our crowns off. And as we now know, the biggest tools the enemy will use are lies and condemnation. The same way he caused Eve to be misled by making her think that she was no longer like God, made in his image and likeness, is the same way he will try to mislead us, causing us to take our crowns off.

Today if you are battling to believe what God has said about you, I want to encourage you to fight for your new identity. Lay hold to what God has said about you and resist the lies of the enemy. The foundation of having a powerful prayer life, one where you can effectively pray for the kingdom of God to come to earth as it is in Heaven, is to know who you really are. You are a king and priest unto our God. You are a joint heir with Christ and you are seated with Him in heavenly places. Don't let anyone steal from you the new identity that Christ has given you as His bride and ekklesia. Don't let anyone take away your crown.

> **The enemy will use anything at his disposal to convince us to take our crowns off.**

> "But I come swiftly, so cling tightly to what you have, so that no one may seize your crown of victory" (Revelation 3:11 TPT).

THE KEYS: OUR AUTHORITY TO OPEN AND SHUT

God has not only given us the irreplaceable gift of a new identity, one that empowers our prayers like nothing can, but He has also given us keys. Keys of kingdom authority to unlock and open, and also to shut and lock up. As with our crown, these keys are not physical but are spiritual. They may only be a spiritual picture that represents the authority we have been given, but they powerfully represent genuine kingdom authority that has been given to the followers of Christ.

Most Christians recognize these keys when Peter confesses Jesus as the Christ, the son of the living God. As Peter makes it clear who *Jesus* is, Jesus makes it clear who *Peter* is. And not just Peter, but the church he will help lead and build. That means we are beneficiaries of the promise Jesus gave to Peter.

> "And I also say to you that you are Peter, and on this rock I will build My church, and the gates of Hades shall not prevail against it. And I will give you the keys of the kingdom of heaven, and whatever you bind on earth will be bound in heaven, and whatever you loose on earth will be loosed in heaven." (Matthew 16:18-19).

When Jesus entrusted those keys to Peter, He also entrusted them to us. If you go back and read books about church history, you will learn the church was empowered to get through some of the most difficult times ever recorded. Leading the early church through the darkness of that lost world took supernatural power and the ability to carry out Heaven's plans and mandates on earth. That is why they needed the keys, and why we need them as well.

KEYS REPRESENT AUTHORITY

Keys represent authority. If someone has been given the key to a door in a building then, in essence, they have been given authority over that office. Even if it's only a janitor. They may not have the key to the private desk of the CEO of that office, but they have been given authority to enter the office to clean it. When anyone has been given a "master key," then that person has authority over the entire office, as the master key will open every door.

I never will forget right after I received my driver's license, my dad gave me the keys to the spare car so that I could drive to school. The thought that I was totally in control of that vehicle, a 1966 Buick Skylark with a 310 Wildcat Engine, was extremely invigorating and also a little scary. I had the keys and that meant I was in charge and had full authority over that car when I drove it to school or football practice. I had the full authority, that is, until a state trooper pulled me over. Just like that I went from teenage heaven to losing my keys for a week. Nothing can be harder for a teenager who just got his wings to make that long walk to the end of the road to catch that yellowbird bus. I had the authority, but just like that I had lost it.

In the kingdom of God, there are all kinds of keys for all kinds of purposes but they all are linked to both authority and ability. I like to think that every key has been cut from the "Master's key." While Jesus gave the keys to the kingdom of Heaven to Peter (and ultimately the church), this was not the first time that keys had been given to man. To see where keys first existed you have to go all the way back to Genesis.

> Then God said, "Let Us make man in Our image, according to Our likeness; let them have dominion over the fish of the sea, over the birds of the air, and over the cattle, over all the earth and over every creeping thing that creeps on the earth." So God created man in His own image; in the image of God He created him; male and female He created them. Then God blessed them, and God said to them, "Be fruitful and multiply; fill the earth and subdue it; have dominion over the fish of the sea, over the birds of the air, and over every living thing that moves on the earth." (Genesis 1:26-28).

Adam and Eve had been given the keys to the Garden of Eden and ultimately the whole earth. In another sign that they were in charge, it states in Genesis 2:15 that after God created Adam, He placed him in the garden to *tend* and *keep* it. In other words, they were put in charge of cultivating and guarding it.

They ultimately failed to guard it as the serpent deceived Eve, and like me after my encounter with the state trooper, they lost the keys to the garden. Thankfully, when I lost my keys (temporarily of course), they went into the hands of my dad. When Adam and Eve lost the keys to the garden those keys were lost into the hands of the serpent.

While Satan did not have the authority to use those keys as God had designed them, He still held the stolen authority.

While it can be complicated to fully understand all that happened in the fall, there is an easier way to explain what happened. In the beginning, Adam and Eve were given the keys. They lost them to the serpent but thankfully God knew well before He created Adam and Eve that they would lose the keys, and He would have to create a plan to get them back again. Thankfully, God had a plan to not only get the keys back, but also the family He had purposed to have. That plan was through the work of His Son, Jesus Christ, who through His death and resurrection took back the keys. Those keys were then given to Peter and the church that Christ would build through Peter.

WE NOW HAVE THE KEYS

This all means that we have been given the keys of the kingdom of Heaven. While that truth can be embraced it does bring up the following questions:

- What are the keys?
- How are they utilized?
- What do the keys do?

KEYS LOCK AND UNLOCK

Before I talk about what the keys are or how they are utilized, I want to share what they do. The keys of the kingdom of Heaven can best be understood by thinking of your house key. Your house key gives you two choices. You can unlock and then open the door, or you can shut and then lock the door. The keys of the kingdom basically do the same thing. They can "open or shut" or they can "loose or bind." Other descriptions give the picture of "releasing or forbidding." The keys of the kingdom of Heaven represent our authority to unlock and release the kingdom of Heaven on earth. They also represent our authority to close and lock the door of access for the kingdom of darkness.

HOW DO WE USE THE KEYS OF AUTHORITY?

This may seem too simple to be so spiritually powerful, but the keys are anything God directs you to do, primarily through prayer but also in action. Remember, the keys represent our connection to kingdom authority in Heaven; authority that is being translated to earth through us, His church. The power to open or close on earth comes from what God has already established in Heaven, not from what we desire to open or close. Anything we do that opens a door or closes a door is a key of authority.

THE KEY OF ACTION

The primary way these keys are appropriated is through our mouth, as we make prayers and decrees based on the leading of the Holy Spirit and the Word of God. There are also many other ways they are used. For instance, I believe I have a key for releasing the love of God. Many times, this key is used through acts of kindness. I visit a person who is greatly discouraged, and just by visiting I am releasing the joy of Heaven here on earth. It has already been established, but I am being sent to open the blinds and let the sunshine in to that place of darkness. While this action is a key in itself, it never goes alone.

THE KEY OF PRAYER

The first way we can use the keys of the kingdom is through the work of prayer. God has given us the ability through prayer to open and close doors. All throughout God's Word we can see how prayer was used to lock and unlock.

Moses' intercession unlocked the mercy of God for Israel after they had made a golden calf and worshiped it.

Esther's prayers were used to shut and lock the door on Haman's evil plot to destroy Mordecai and all of the Jews.

Daniel's prayers not only unlocked and opened the door of revelation, showing him things that were to come, but they also were indirectly used to shut and lock the mouths of a bunch of hungry lions.

The prayers of the church were used to unlock and open the doors of the prison so that Peter could would be set free. Have you ever realized that your keys of prayer could be indirectly used to employ the work of angels? You might pray for someone to be released from the grip of a chemical addiction, and God uses angels to assist in shutting the door to access the drugs.

A WALL COMES DOWN

In the early 1980's, I can remember hearing several Christian leaders praying for the Berlin Wall to come down. At the time, Germany was divided between East Germany and West Germany, with East Germany experiencing all the evils of communism as they were aligned with the Soviet Union. It truly was the tale of two cities: West Berlin being built on capitalism, while East Berlin was held back by communism.

Those Christian leaders prayed, asking God to remove the wall so the gospel of Christ could be freely preached in East Germany without any barriers to hold it back.

On November 9th, 1989, those prayers began to be answered as the citizens of both West and East Germany started tearing down the wall. While there was a lot of political work that went into seeing Germany reunified, there is no doubt that keys were being used to tear down that wall. Those keys not only tore down a wall, but more importantly opened up a door for freedom and the spread of the gospel throughout

East Germany. As is the case with many open doors, that opening continued to bring forth light, and shortly after, the Soviet Union, as we knew it, was dissolved.

You may be looking at an impossible situation, one that would take an army or a decision by the Supreme Court. No matter what you are facing, God has given you the keys. Keys, through His direction, that can open or close any door.

HOW TO USE KEYS IN PRAYER

Pray about it. The first thing you should do is talk to God about it. As you approach prayer, it's important that you begin with the source of prayer, which is God. If Praying for Reign is more about God getting our attention than us getting His, then it's important for us to find out what He is saying. Personally, I ask God, "What are the keys and how do I use them?" God knows, and He is more than willing to direct me.

Obey what God has said. God has not only spoken through His Word, but is now speaking through His Holy Spirit. God's Word is a primary source for gaining wisdom on how to pray and how to use the keys. The Bible is filled with directions on how and what to pray for in almost any given situation imaginable. In the end, the Bible will be your ultimate authority when making a stand in faith. The Bible is filled with keys that you have the full authority to pray with.

Ask the Holy Spirit to guide you. The voice of God that comes through His Holy Spirit can guide us on how to pray. Sometimes prayer can become difficult to chart. The Holy Spirit is the "Locksmith of Prayer," and when I don't know how to approach opening a door or closing one, I call for His help.

Don't look for ultimate results; look for breakthrough. When you are praying for a door to be open or for one to be shut, it's important to position yourself for the long haul and pray until your prayer is answered or you receive other direction. To persevere through a lot of potential discourage-ment and delays, it's important to look for little breakthroughs. The men

> The Holy Spirit is the "Locksmith of Prayer," and when I don't know how to approach opening a door or closing one, I call for His help.

and women who have been praying for the overturning of *Roe v. Wade* had to look for little breakthroughs and encouragement along the way. It might have been just one decision, by one judge, in one state, but if you are going to stay with it you will need to take encouragement from Heaven and little breakthroughs.

Don't overlook small keys. Those who prayed for the Berlin Wall to come down may have never imagined it would be the beginning of the dissolution of the Soviet Union, but it was. Your prayer to open a door of kingdom into one neighbor's heart could lead to opening

> Little keys can open big doors.

a door to the entire neighborhood. Little keys can open big doors.

THE SWORD: THE MOST POWERFUL WEAPON WE HAVE

While it's important to know our position and the authority we have been given in prayer, it is just as vital to know the weapons we have been given in order to pray effectively. There are all kinds of var-ious weapons to enhance and empower prayer—things like fasting and even silence—but there is one weapon that is irreplicable. That weapon is the Word of God.

We've covered the tools I was given as a state trooper, but we also had several weapons we could use to accomplish our job of serving and protecting the public. The use of a weapon or the use of force had to follow what was called the "Use of Force Continuum." The Use of Force Continuum is a standard that provides law enforcement officers with guidelines as to how much force may be used against a resisting subject in any given situation. It begins at the lowest use of force needed and moves to the highest, most serious level, which calls for the use of your firearm.

What might surprise you is that the use of force begins with just your presence. The presence of a law enforcement officer is lowest form of the use of force. The greatest hope of any true servant of peace would be that just their presence would be enough to solve any situation they're responding to. It's the dream of every law enforcement officer that just by showing up, a fight will stop, and every person who is wanted will just turn themselves in peacefully. As we move forward in our authority in prayer it all begins with us taking a stand or by just showing up. Before any spiritual weapons can be used in prayer, we must be present and engaged.

As it is in the natural, so it is in the spiritual. We have been given weapons to be able to follow Christ in extending His kingdom. Obviously, there are many weapons that (when combined with prayer) produce amazing results, but none quite like the Word of God.

Why is the Word of God, the Sword of The Spirit, so important in empowering our prayers? There are three major things that the Word of God does that empowers our prayers to a whole new level.

The sword is faith-building. The Word of God builds our faith. Faith is one of the most important elements for having a strong foundation for prayer.

The sword establishes our authority. It is one thing if we are making things up on our own when battling in prayer (that's never a good idea), but when we are standing on God's Word, we have biblical authority. The Word of the Lord empowers our authority in prayer like nothing else can.

Recognized by God. It's God's Word, so when it is used properly, He accepts it based upon the merits that it came from Him. Nothing gives me greater confidence than praying the very promises and words of God.

The Sword reminds God of His promises. I love what is said in Isaiah 62:6-7 (NASB):

On your walls, O Jerusalem, I have appointed watchmen;
All day and all night they will never keep silent.
You who remind the Lord, take no rest for yourselves;
And give Him no rest until He establishes
And makes Jerusalem a praise in the earth.

Clearly, in this portion of scripture God is commanding us to stand on the wall and intercede, to remind Him—but remind him of what? While God never forgets, He does direct us to remind Him of something. This can only mean one thing: we are to remind Him of His Word and His promises. The sword enables us to do just that.

All of these tools are vital to prayer. When they are coupled with the work of the Holy Spirit, it's like you put them into God's hands as He works through you by His Spirit. This makes the Holy Spirit our most powerful partner in prayer.

Chapter Eleven

THE HOLY SPIRIT

Your Greatest Partner in Praying for Reign

AUDIENCE WITH A KING

While our prayers can be directed to any member of the Trinity, it's important to see why Jesus directed His disciples to pray to our Heavenly Father in the Lord's Prayer. Hidden in this picture and many other teachings throughout the Word of God is a beautiful picture of the pattern of prayer and how the entire Trinity is involved when we pray.

The pattern for prayer is that our prayers funnel up to our Heavenly Father, through the Son, with the help and guidance of the Holy Spirit.

As you think about that, it paints a beautiful picture of how the entire God-head is working together to help us have a powerful and impactful prayer life. When I tell you God is committed to helping you Pray for Reign, nothing displays this more than understanding that the Trinity is working together to assist you. You are not praying alone.

Below are some further points to help this pattern of prayer become clearer. Again, our prayers could be addressed to Jesus, the Holy Spirit, or directly to the Father. Since they are all one, our prayer is headed in the right direction, so don't get hung up on absolutes. This is about revelation, not rituals or form. With that said, when we can understand the principle of this order it helps us see how the whole God-head, the Trinity, is involved in our prayers. Again, work to understand the truth, not to develop a ritual.

- The destination of our prayers is our Heavenly Father.
- Jesus is the Way, so our prayers have access to the Father through Him.
- The Holy Spirit is our helper and our guide.

Now let's look at it even deeper as I share a beautiful illustration God revealed to me about how prayer is like being granted an audience with a king.

HOLY SPIRIT: THE PRIVATE SECRETARY TO THE KING

Imagine you are about to have an audience with a king. Before you approach the throne, someone helps prepare you before walking into the king's presence. This person is usually the private secretary of the king or their appointee.

There are a lot of "royal protocols" to follow when you have an audience with a king, and this person will make sure you know and follow them all. Their job is to prepare you so your audience is successful. In this kind of an audience, they are your best friend and your ally.

After the private secretary has helped you prep for your audience, they will lead you through the doorway directly into the throne room. They will always announce you as you enter the king's presence so the king knows who you are. They not only go with you, but on many occasions, they will even speak on your behalf to make sure the king understands your request or the nature of your audience. They are there to help you.

This special assistant for us is the Holy Spirit. He not only prepares us before we pray, but He also helps us when we do not know how to pray. He is more than just a guide; He is our "paraclete." That means, according to most biblical dictionaries, He is our:

- Legal advocate
- Intercessor
- Helper

I like to say that the Holy Spirit is our greatest prayer partner. With His help, we can navigate prayer without a single worry that we are going to miss something or flub it up. Without Him, we would be like someone wandering through Buckingham Palace trying to find our way to where the king is actually located.

The Holy Spirit is the key to us understanding prayer, especially the Lord's Prayer. He is the one who will take the outline and fill in all the blanks. He moves it from a beautiful, but often ritualistic, prayer to a powerful revelation for prayer breakthrough.

The Holy Spirit is the guide. Next is the One who has made a way for us to enter and access the Father.

JESUS: THE GRAND DOOR OF ACCESS

In my illustration, the door that leads to the king and His throne room goes through Jesus. Imagine your guide as He walks you up to the doorway. The door is open wide to you; it's open wide because Christ has opened it for you and me, and every other believer who has been born again.

Jesus is the way, our point of access, and it was through His blood that we have this unlimited access to our King and Heavenly Father. There is an open-door policy with the Heavenly Father for all of us who are called children of God, but it comes through Jesus. If you will, imagine that Jesus is like your best friend, but since He is the Son of the King, you have access to the King through your friendship with the Son. That is the type of access we have to the Father.

It's amazing to think that upon one's repentance and being born again, this door is opened wide. While it's true that Jesus is seated at the right hand of God, He also is the doorway to this very special relationship we have with our Heavenly Father. There are no other doors to this relationship outside of Jesus.

OUR HEAVENLY FATHER: ABBA GOD

Beyond the access or doorway of Christ, we enter the throne room of the King, not just the King, but also our Heavenly Father, our Abba. The meaning of Abba, an Aramaic word, is "Father." It was a common term that not only expressed affection but also confidence and trust. Because this word signifies a close, intimate relationship between a father and his child, we know we can boldly approach the throne. In fact, we can crawl up into His lap. There is no fear that He will not extend the scepter, as in the story of Queen Esther. You are never bothering Him when you approach His throne.

PRAYING WITH THE TRINITY

Can you picture this scene with me? When you are entering into spirit-led prayer, you are being prepared by and led by the Holy Spirit into the throne room of God. Together with the Spirit, you make your way through the door of access that has been provided by the Son. Jesus not only provides you that access, He is also present when you approach the throne. Imagine this: when you pray, you are in that throne room standing before your Heavenly Father and you are surrounded by the Holy Spirit and Jesus. It's a powerful and a very

> **Prayer is to the Father, through the Son, with the help and guidance of the Holy Spirit.**

accurate picture of what occurs when we are praying spirit-led prayers. I have often reminded myself that when I pray, there are four people in the fire and this time I am that fourth person. Again, prayer is to the Father, through the Son, with the help and guidance of the Holy Spirit.

The importance of learning this is so we can understand that God has already done everything for us to have a powerful and vibrant prayer life. It does not matter if you are a stay-at-home mom, a retired person, or a business owner. You have the same access your pastor has. God has provided the way and even provided us a powerful outline for prayer in the Lord's Prayer.

The most important point everyone should get from this part is that the Holy Spirit is an absolute invaluable partner when it comes to prayer. Praying with and through the assistance of the Holy Spirit can turn the meekest man or woman of prayer into a modern-day Elijah or Daniel. The Holy Spirit is your guide, your friend, your interpreter, your advocate, and legal aid. No one can help you enter into prayer like He can.

> Praying with and through the assistance of the Holy Spirit can turn the meekest man or woman of prayer into a modern-day Elijah or Daniel.

How can I pray with the Holy Spirit?

- Ask
- Listen
- Follow

We Ask. When I begin to enter prayer, I simply say, "Holy Spirit, I need your help on knowing how to pray for these things." Or I may say, "Holy Spirit, I sense there are some things I need to pray about. Can you help me understand what they are and lead me?"

Now at times I might say Jesus instead of Holy Spirit, and that's okay, but I know I am asking for the help of His Spirit that lives within me. The most important thing is that I am asking. I love the promises of God that are built around asking.

> So it is with your prayers. Ask and you'll receive. Seek and you'll discover. Knock on Heaven's door, and it will one day open for you. Every persistent person will receive what he asks for. Every persistent seeker will discover what he needs. And everyone who knocks persistently will one day find an open door.

> Let me ask you this: Do you know of any father who would give his son a snake on a plate when he asked for a serving of fish? Of course not! Do you know of any father who would give his daughter a spider when she had asked for an egg? Of course not! If imperfect parents know how to lovingly take care of their children and give them what they need, how much more will the perfect heavenly Father give the Holy Spirit's fullness when his children ask him. Luke 11:11-13 (TPT)

> Ask me and I will tell you remarkable secrets you do not know about things to come. Jeremiah 33:3 (NLT)

WHY DO WE NEED TO ASK?

The Bible also says we have not because we ask not. Many people misunderstand why we need to ask. Some think it's because God is holding out on us until we come to Him and formally ask. While our Heavenly Father is much like any other father who likes to be asked, it's more than that.

He desires for us to ask because it is necessary. God does not need our permission, but He does seek and require our agreement. In His sovereign design He has given us a free will. In the end He will not violate His word, nor His promises to keep His word.

God will do everything possible to woo us and move us toward Him, but we need to ask. Even with salvation, He will not force it on any man or woman. His Holy Spirit will work to convict and draw everyone to Jesus, but in the end, everyone must believe in their heart and confess with their mouth that Jesus is Lord and that God raised Him from the dead. Asking for help is not a sign of weakness; it's actually a sign of incredible strength.

> **Asking for help is not a sign of weakness, it's actually a sign of incredible strength.**

We Listen. Did you know the Holy Spirit loves to speak to us, that He is the voice of God on earth? When Jesus said it was good that He should go away, it was not so we would be alone. On the contrary, He sent His Spirit so the Holy Spirit could dwell in each of us.

The Holy Spirit loves to speak to us, but we have to be willing to hear Him. In a world full of so much noise and daily distractions, His voice can be drowned out if we are not careful. He also is very sensitive. If you would like to discover more about that concept, one of my favorite authors, R. T. Kendal, writes about this unique sensitivity in his book *Sensitivity of the Spirit*. The first time I read it, I was moved to see the Holy Spirit in a very different light. I am so thankful for the Holy Spirit.

As you read through the Bible you can see how He speaks to the church, directing them and guiding them. The New Testament is full of stories of the Holy Spirit as He works side-by-side with the church. It's clear that Jesus directed the church to wait on His promise, the promise of the Holy Spirit, because without it they would have been very lost. But just read how the Holy Spirit directed the church.

Now an angel of the Lord spoke to Philip, saying, "Arise and go toward the south along the road which goes down from Jerusalem to Gaza." This is desert. So he arose and went. And behold, a man of Ethiopia, a eunuch of great authority under Candace the queen of the Ethiopians, who had charge of all her treasury, and had come to Jerusalem to worship, was returning. And sitting in his chariot, he was reading Isaiah the prophet. **Then the Spirit said to Philip**, "Go near and overtake this chariot." So Philip ran to him, and heard him reading the prophet Isaiah, and said, "Do you understand what you are reading?" Acts 8:26-30

As they ministered to the Lord and fasted, **the Holy Spirit said**, "Now separate to Me Barnabas and Saul for the work to which I have called them." [3] Then, having fasted and prayed, and laid hands on them, they sent *them* away. Acts 13:2-3

Jesus made it plain that when He went away, the Spirit would come and would speak to us.

"I still have many things to say to you, but you cannot bear *them* now. However, when He, the Spirit of truth, has come, He will guide you into all truth; for He will not speak on His own *authority*, but whatever He hears He will speak; and He will tell you things to come." John 16:12-13

We Follow. I told the story earlier in the book about when the Holy Spirit directed me to ask God to bless me at a job I really hated. In the end He blessed me greatly, but none of that would have ever happened if I would have been unwilling to do what He asked me to do. It's important to ask and listen, but it is vital to follow and obey.

Has God directed you to do something you still have not done? While we cannot always go back and complete the things God asked us to do in the past, there may still be time to obey His last instruction. Just ask Him. If not, then ask Him what you should do next and with His new direction take a step forward.

I could tell you several personal stories of how important it is to follow God's direction once you've received it. Through each of them I have come to learn a valuable lesson, the lesson that delayed obedience is often really just disobedience.

> I could tell you several personal stories of how important it is to follow God's direction once you received it. Through each of them I have come to learn a valuable lesson, the lesson that delayed obedience is often really just disobedience.

I thank God for His wonderful grace which has allowed me several second and third chances to obey His direction when I didn't go at first. Thankfully we can learn from our past mistakes and learn to trust His voice to follow His direction.

DON'T OUTRUN THE HELPER

Most of us live in the "fast lane" of life. We work long hours and are almost always in a hurry. The pace of our life can push us to move at such speed that it seems almost imposable to slow down to listen.

I will never forget something that happened to me a few years back. It was a chain of events that led to a very powerful realization, one I needed. I had been in a very busy season of life, one with meetings and deadlines piling up like leaves in the peak of fall. It was during this season that someone had given me an amazing book titled *Soul Keeping* by John Ortberg. I really did not have time to read it, but I found just enough time to thumb through it. All it took was reading one statement on one page and just like that I was hooked. I became aware that I was suffering from "hurry sickness."

I often tell people it's not so much reading the right book that changes your life, as it is reading the right statement, on the right page, in the right book, at the right time. This was that moment for me and I am so thankful John Ortberg wrote that book as it was the beginning of a turn in my life, a turn to stop being in such a hurry.

AN ENCOUNTER WITH THE HOLY SPIRIT

Later that year, I traveled with my wife Tracee to Tallahassee to attend a Florida State University football game. We had decided to spend the night after the game and the only hotel we could find was just north of Tallahassee in Thomasville, Georgia. Since it was a Saturday night game, we stayed that night and planned to travel home on Sunday afternoon. The next morning when we woke up, I went downstairs to get a cup of coffee. When I returned to our room, I sat down in the one chair, located by the window.

The window I was sitting in front of faced the back of the hotel property, which was adjacent to a farm. It was very cold that morning and I was looking at the frost on the roof of the barn just a short distance away. The early sunlight seemed to dance across the roof as it shimmered on the blanket of frost from the night before.

As I was caught by the beautiful view, I could hear hunting dogs off in the distance barking. For over a half an hour, I just stared at that roof and, believe it or not, I actually thought of nothing. I didn't think about breakfast or the game my team had lost the night before. I didn't think about meeting up with my children for brunch. I actually thought of nothing. All I did was sip my coffee and look at the frost.

In that moment I experienced one of the most complete moments of peace of my entire life. It was like my soul was being repaired, second by ticking second. Only later on did I realize that I had experienced the presence of God through His Holy Spirit. Did He say anything profound, or tell me to do something? No, I was in His presence and that was enough. While nothing was spoken to me, a lot was communicated.

We always think it takes noise to communicate something, but how many times is something communicated when nothing is said at all? I can only think of the command in Psalm 46:10: "Be still, and know that I *am* God."

I tell this story to help you understand how much the business of the world can keep us from experiencing and hearing from God through His Holy Spirit. The Holy Spirit is not just a part of the Trinity, He also is a person who is our helper and guide. I often think how many times I have passed Him by, too busy to stop to ask, listen, and follow.

Using the illustration that I shared earlier, I compare the Holy Spirit to the king's private secretary, the one who will not only prepare you but guide you through your audience with the Sovereign. Imagine if you passed right by Him without stopping and just kept walking into the palace on your own. You could be lost for hours and end up missing your appointment with the king. I think of how many times I prayed amiss and it really came down to not waiting on the guidance and direction of the Holy Spirit.

THE HOLY SPIRIT IN THE COURT OF HEAVEN

One time when I was praying, I found myself praying in the court of Heaven. If this is new to you, I invite you to not only search it out in scripture, but there are many teachers in the body of Christ who teach about this truth. I personally recommend Robert Henderson. His books and teachings have helped me tremendously.

On this particular day, I was walking the property where the old church had once stood that my great-great uncle and aunt had pastored in downtown Orlando. The church they had planted had long been gone, but the effects of the church and their ministry live on to this day. As I shared earlier in this book, my great-great-aunt Epsie was known as a prayer warrior with a great influence for the kingdom of God.

I had walked the property in the past, praying for my prayers and her prayers to connect in hopes of seeing revival come to Central Florida. I know she prayed for it, as I do now.

On this day, I walked and prayed but felt a strong resistance to my prayers. As I continued to pray, I felt led to pray that the past would be healed. I kept feeling that something had happened in the past that had caused a curse to come upon the land. What could it have been? Who really knows. It could have been a church split where people held unforgiveness for years. I could only tell that something had happened and it needed to be made right.

This revelation moved me to pray that whatever curses were caused would be broken. I was standing in the gap on behalf of others to remove the curse from the past, and release the flow and power of my ancestor's prayers, as well as many others. I felt that I was praying correctly when all of a sudden, I heard this:

"You have no right to ask for that."

"If others brought the curse then they have to be the ones to repent for it."

"You have no rights here."

While it was not an audible voice, it was just as strong. My spiritual life is guided and directed by my faith, God's Word, and the voice of the Lord as He leads me and speaks to me through His Spirit. What I heard this day was not the voice of the Lord and I knew that without any doubt. This was the voice of the enemy. *Why would he be speaking to me,* I thought, and just like that I knew that I was in the courtroom of Heaven.

> **I may have been circling that city block in prayer on the outside, but inside I was praying in a different place.**

I may have been circling that city block in prayer on the outside, but inside I was praying in a different place.

One of the many attributes I love about God is that He is just. This means He will always act in a way that is just. As Judge, God not only settles disputes, but more importantly He makes judgements and rulings. I truly believe this is the whole reason why God allows the accuser of the brethren to come before Him to make accusations regarding His children. If He refused to allow it, then He would not be just. If He stopped being just, He would stop being God, which He can never do.

The voice I heard that day was of the enemy. In an attempt to discourage me and drive me away from praying, He inserted an argument in the midst of my intercession. If you could just imagine a courtroom where the opposing attorney objects to your testimony, that's exactly what it felt like. Being a former law enforcement officer, I have found myself testifying in court more than I care to remember.

The enemy is constantly trying to interrupt and object to our prayers. In most cases, I can depend on the testimony of Jesus' blood that represents me. The enemy attacks my prayer with condemnation, telling me I have no right to pray since I had recently sinned in one way or another. Thankfully the blood of Jesus and His covenant testifies on my behalf.

> And we have come to Jesus who established a new covenant with his blood sprinkled upon the mercy seat; blood that continues to speak from heaven, "forgiveness," a better message than Abel's blood that cries from the earth, "justice." Hebrews 12:24 (TPT)

Thankfully, I can always have a case of the enemy's dismissed by God if I have truly repented of my sin. He is always forced to withdraw his accusation and lies when I stand on the testimony of Jesus.

While I can always have arguments against me dismissed if I am standing on the promises of God, it can be much more difficult when you are trying to break a curse that others may have caused over seventy years ago. It would have been totally different if I had attended this church where my great-great-uncle and aunt were the pastors—I would then be a representative from that group—but my only connection was my relatives.

The voice I heard in my spirit was making a good point. How could an outsider step in and spiritually correct someone else's error? What could I interject that would allow me to approach the bench of Heaven and submit an argument to overrule the enemy's claim?

Honestly, I had no idea what to do next. I thought about getting back into my truck and driving home. Retreat to regather my thoughts to hopefully return on another day. But I decided to wait. I waited until I felt directed to ask the Holy Spirit for His help. One of the words that describes the Holy Spirit is "Advocate." This means that the Holy Spirit is our legal assistant and counsel for our defense.

Have you ever had a serious legal question? Did you go and ask your car mechanic or the mailman for advice? Of course you didn't. You made an appointment to talk with a lawyer, someone who understood the law and could also represent you if needed to go to court.

On this day I was already in court, looking for any ground to stand on so I could pray against the past curse that I felt was blocking God from answering my prayers. I prayed and asked the Holy Spirit to help me. I kept walking around the property, praying and waiting on my Counselor to help me. I had no idea what He was going to say; I had never done this before. It was then that I heard "David and Goliath." I thought to myself, "Yes, I feel like David battling the stronghold of Goliath," but I knew that was not it.

I just kept walking and waiting, waiting for more revelation. Then it came to me in one quick but powerful download. When David defeated Goliath, the Philistines were basically occupying land that belonged to Judah. For forty days they stood opposite of Israel, sending out Goliath to challenge them. The revelation that came to me was that David did not cause the situation; it was happening because the army of Israel was paralyzed with fear. David was not even present when it started; it really was King Saul's issue, as well as David's brother's issue. As I continued to meditate on this, it became crystal clear: God used

David to bring deliverance, despite the fact that the situation was not caused by David's disobedience or fear. His one connection to it was to the land. The land that the Philistines were illegally occupying was the land of Judah, David's family.

What the Holy Spirit counseled me to do was to use "legal precedence" and submit my argument to remove the curses I sensed, solely based upon this argument. If God could use David to remove a curse from land that had belonged to his family, then God could use me to remove this one. As I prayed with the insight that Holy Spirit had just given me, the change was immediate. I spent the next half hour praying under an open Heaven, breaking curses and releasing light as I prayed for revival to come to Orlando.

The Holy Spirit is not just our prayer partner, He also is our legal aid. When you have a difficult situation that seems to evade your prayers no matter how hard you pray, it's time to turn to the Counselor. He is always available and ready to step in to advise you and represent you.

If God could use David to remove a curse from land that had belonged to his family, then God could use me to remove this one.

For us to truly partner with and agree with God through prayer for the fulfillment of His plan—His plan to manifest His kingdom realm on earth as it is in Heaven—then we need the help of the Holy Spirit. The Holy Spirit is here to help us Pray for Reign.

Chapter Twelve

WHEN GOD CALLS

*Praying for Reign through Prayer Journeys
and Prayer Assignments*

A s God prepares you and calls you to Pray for Reign, His call for you to join Him in prayer can be manifested in two ways. The first is in Prayer Assignments, and the second is Prayer Journeys.

PRAYER ASSIGNMENTS

Just as it sounds, these are things assigned to you specifically. While prayer assignments can come out of the Word of God, some come through a calling or divine revelation.

The prayer assignments that come out of God's Word are standard for all of us. For example, every Christian should pray for their leaders as it is commanded in scripture.

> Therefore I exhort first of all that supplications, prayers, intercessions, *and* giving of thanks be made for all men, for kings and all who are in authority, that we may lead a quiet and peaceable life in all godliness and reverence.

> For this *is* good and acceptable in the sight of God our Savior. 1 Timothy 2:1-3

As Christians, we do not need a special assignment to know that we are to pray for our leaders, both in government and anyone else who is given authority to lead. That being said, to be called to pray for one particular leader can be an assignment.

> **As Christians, we do not need a special assignment to know that we are to pray for our leaders, both in government and anyone else who is given authority to lead.**

Prayer assignments can be for people, places, and even things. Have you ever felt assigned to pray for rain? That it was just more than a need you observed, it was a calling to do so? It's not that unusual to have those types of assignments. Elijah had that very assignment from God: to pray for rain.

> The effective, fervent prayer of a righteous man avails much. Elijah was a man with a nature like ours, and he prayed earnestly that it would not rain; and it did not rain on the land for three years and six months. And he prayed again, and the heaven gave rain, and the earth produced its fruit. James 5:16b-18

You can read this entire story in 1 Kings chapter eighteen. Elijah wasn't turning off the rain because he wanted to get back at King Ahab. He also was not turning it back on again because it was too dry after it had not rained for three years and six months. Elijah did it because he had a prayer assignment from God.

> **Prayer assignments can be for people, places, and even things.**

These assignments can also be for specific people. Just look at the story of Ananias in the book of Acts:

Now there was a certain disciple at Damascus named Ananias; and to him the Lord said in a vision, "Ananias."

And he said, "Here I am, Lord."

So the Lord said to him, "Arise and go to the street called Straight, and inquire at the house of Judas for one called Saul of Tarsus, for behold, he is praying. And in a vision he has seen a man named Ananias coming in and putting his hand on him, so that he might receive his sight."

Then Ananias answered, "Lord, I have heard from many about this man, how much harm he has done to Your saints in Jerusalem. And here he has authority from the chief priests to bind all who call on Your name."

But the Lord said to him, "Go, for he is a chosen vessel of Mine to bear My name before Gentiles, kings, and the children of Israel. For I will show him how many things he must suffer for My name's sake."

And Ananias went his way and entered the house; and laying his hands on him he said, "Brother Saul, the Lord Jesus, who appeared to you on the road as you came, has sent me that you may receive your sight and be filled with the Holy Spirit." Immediately there fell from his eyes something like scales, and he received his sight at once; and he arose and was baptized. Acts 9:10-18

Ananias' assignment was to go and lay hands on Saul of Tarsus, that he would receive his sight and be filled with the Holy Spirit. Looking at this story, we also learn that sometimes assignments will lead us to pray for people we may not like.

Another example of a prayer assignment from God would be that of Job.

> And so it was, after the LORD had spoken these words to Job, that the LORD said to Eliphaz the Temanite, "My wrath is aroused against you and your two friends, for you have not spoken of Me *what is* right, as My servant Job *has*. Now therefore, take for yourselves seven bulls and seven rams, go to My servant Job, and offer up for yourselves a burnt offering; and My servant Job shall pray for you. For I will accept him, lest I deal with you *according to your* folly; because you have not spoken of Me *what is* right, as My servant Job *has*."
>
> So Eliphaz the Temanite and Bildad the Shuhite *and* Zophar the Naamathite went and did as the LORD commanded them; for the LORD had accepted Job. And the LORD restored Job's losses when he prayed for his friends. Indeed the LORD gave Job twice as much as he had before. Job 42:7-10

Here are a few things to know about prayer assignments

- They are specific.
- They can last a day or last years. You generally pray until it is answered or you are released.
- They can often be for things we would not normally pray for.
- They do not always come with the same emotion we have for our own request.
- They can be for people, places, and things.
- The assignment originates with God.

- They require the guidance of the Holy Spirit.

HOW DO YOU KNOW IF YOU HAVE RECEIVED A PRAYER ASSIGNMENT?

While there is not always a clear way to know for sure, here are some guidelines. They will help you determine if you have received one, or if the prayer you have already been praying has elevated to an assignment.

> **The increase of revelation.** Your general prayer for this person, place, or thing begins to become more specific. You begin to receive insight and revelation on how to pray deeper. It moves from just a prayer request to an assignment.

> **Divine direction.** You hear or sense strongly that God is calling you to pray for the person, place, or thing.

> **Prophetic confirmation.** You receive a confirming prophetic word that lets you know this is the target you are to aim for.

> **Increase in desire.** It may have started as just a request, but the desire to pray for that person, place, or thing is not going away; in fact, it's getting stronger.

PRAYER JOURNEYS

Prayer journeys can start similar to prayer assignments in that God will give us either a desire or His direction to go into an area to pray. Prayer journeys can lead to prayer assignments, and they are often attached in one way or another, but journeys are specifically linked to a call to come and see something. Two places in scripture where this occurred was with Abraham, and then with Jesus and His disciples.

One of the greatest examples of this in the Bible is through the life and ministry of Jesus. While no one ever called it a prayer journey, Jesus was leading His disciples through what has been termed by Andrew Murray as the "school of prayer." One of those teaching sessions demonstrates how powerful a prayer journey can be. It comes from the Gospel of Matthew, where Jesus was instructing His disciples regarding the harvest.

> Jesus walked throughout the region with the joyful message of God's kingdom realm. He taught in their meeting houses, and wherever he went he demonstrated God's power by healing every kind of disease and illness. When he saw the vast crowds of people, Jesus' heart was deeply moved with compassion, because they seemed weary and helpless, like wandering sheep without a shepherd. He turned to his disciples and said, "The harvest is huge and ripe! But there are not enough harvesters to bring it all in. As you go, plead with the Owner of the Harvest to thrust out many more reapers to harvest his grain!" Matthew 9:35-38 (TPT)

This is a perfect example of how prayer journeys occur:

- The Lord calls us to follow Him.
- The Lord points something out for us to see.
- He then directs us on how to pray or intercede.
- The experience changes us forever.

I have been on several prayer journeys over the years. Here are two major ones that have impacted me greatly.

MY PRAYER JOURNEY TO WALES

I have taken three trips to Wales in my lifetime. The first was in 2002 when myself, my wife Tracee, and our daughter Ashlee went to be part of a crusade that the late Evangelist Steve Hill was holding in Southern Wales. I told this story earlier in the book; no journey has impacted me quite as much as this one did. Being in the historic epicenter of where the Welsh Revival first began put a lasting mark within my heart and spirit. Twenty years later, I continue to pray for the "Wells of Wales" to reopen again.

On my second trip to Wales, later that same year, I returned home with a small jar of sand. I wanted to bring it home so I could hold it while I prayed for revival to visit this wonderful country once again.

It was on my last trip that God impacted me the most in my calling to pray. In 2004, I returned with Steve Hill to be part of another crusade that coincided with the hundredth anniversary of the Welsh Revival. As part of my duties on this trip, I was to arrange several day trips or tours for the partners of Steve's ministry, who came to be part of the nightly crusades.

> It was life-changing for me to stand in the "Blue Room," and imagine Rees leading his team in prayer during WWII as Germany was threatening England.

One of those day trips took us to the home of Rees Howells, at the Bible College of Wales. The staff was kind enough to give us a full tour of the Bible school while also telling us many stories of what God had done through Rees and his team while they prayed. It was life-changing for me to stand in the "Blue Room," and imagine Rees leading his team in prayer during WWII as Germany was threatening England. While I was there to support my pastor and the efforts of the crusade, God was giving me a whole new assignment for prayer. I often feel like I hold a tiny portion of the mantle that Rees Howells wore. While there are few intercessors who have lived prayer like he did, his life has inspired thousands to give themselves to prayer.

My trips to Wales gave me several prayer assignments that I still carry to this day.

MY PRAYER JOURNEY TO WASHINGTON, D.C.

In the fall of 2019, Tracee and I felt called to go to Washington, D.C., to pray. The desire to go began when Dutch Sheets shared a dream directing him to go to the nation's capital in the spring of 2020 to pray. Listening to that dream put an instant desire to go to Washington in my heart as well, not as part of anything Dutch was doing, but on our own. It was fall of 2019, but for some reason I felt that we should go on March 20, 2020. We booked our tickets and hotel, and looked forward to not only going to D.C. to pray, but also to seeing our daughter Brittnee who lived there at the time.

Just two weeks before our planned trip, the Covid-19 pandemic started triggering panic in the United States. As each day inched closer to our trip, more and more shutdowns were announced. We sought God to see if we were to cancel or go. God said "go." The day we flew into Reagan National Airport, we arrived to a town that was basically shutting down. I am glad we knew without any doubt that we were supposed to go, because everything in the natural pointed to this being the wrong time.

As we began to fulfill our assignment to pray throughout Washington, D.C., for three days, we could sense God's presence in an incredible way. There were times I could not even talk about what I was sensing without choking up. It really seemed as if God Himself was waiting for us to join Him in D.C. Our three days were so incredibly powerful. From praying in front of the White House to praying with my hands pressed against the very doors of the Supreme Court, God was not just recording my prayers in Heaven, He was also recording His desires on my heart.

On the last day I saw a sight which really moved me. As we were completing our prayer walk and heading up the hill to the Washington Monument, I looked up in the clouds and saw what appeared to be a round hole. Stretched all over the sky were those dark clouds that you normally see before a snowfall, except for this one circular hole you could see blue sky through. I always liked to look for shapes in clouds as a young boy, but this was more than just a weather coincidence; it was a confirmation to me. God had given me a word on the first day of this trip that I would pray under an open Heaven. While I did not need the sign in the clouds to know God had been with us, it was a nice exclamation point.

Since that trip, God has assigned me and Tracee to pray for Washington, D.C. All you need to do is visit my home office to know that I now have pictures and maps of Washington, D.C., on several walls. They are strategic prayer maps that not only remind me, but also inspire me, to pray for our nation's capital.

Prayer journeys are significant because God uses them not only to direct my prayers, but more importantly to direct me. While these journeys take time and money, if God is putting one on your heart, you should make it a matter of prayer. Prayer journeys are much like visiting the front line of a battle. You can't truly know what is going on until you see it for yourself.

> **Prayer journeys are much like visiting the front line of a battle. You can't truly know what is going on until you see it for yourself.**

I believe this is why Jesus asked His disciples to look at the people in Matthew chapter nine. By seeing them close and upfront, they would not only know their need better, they would also know their Master's heart better. Seeing is not always believing, but it's quite often understanding. God leads us to the front row so we can see what is on His heart. In the end, true prayer assignments come from a willingness to not only see what is on the Father's heart but also being willing to help carry it. In the story of

> **In the story of the Prodigal Son, the elder brother would have had a completely different reaction to his brother's homecoming if he had taken on the assignment to pray for his brother's return.**

the Prodigal Son, the elder brother would have had a completely different reaction to his brother's homecoming if he had taken on the assignment to pray for his brother's return.

WHY GO?

Many times, people ask me, "Why do you need to go on a prayer journey? Can't you pray from home?" The answer to that question is always "yes," but there are some key reasons why you should go on a prayer journey.

Obedience. The most important reason to go is because God has called you to. Whether you sense anything while you're there or not, going is the right thing to do if you know God has called you to go.

Praying on-site with insight. Praying on location offers two benefits. First, it's a faith-multiplier for empowering and directing your prayers. Second, you will pick up spiritual intel by being on site. It's one thing to see pictures of the Supreme Court; it's another thing to put your hands on the front doors.

It's God's pattern. God has many times moved people to specific places to pray or experience Him for His purposes. An example would be Jacob returning to Bethel and Moses leading Israel to Mt. Sinai.

Responding to a prophetic word. Following the call of God through His Word, through a prophetic word, or a dream is not only an act of faith but also one of obedience.

Remove the distractions. Finally, prayer journeys are able to remove us from the distractions and routines of our daily lives.

They give us the ability to pull aside and gain a single focus. While we can pray from home for the President, it's a whole different thing doing it in front of the White House.

IN CONCLUSION

I challenge you to pray about taking a prayer journey of your own. Even if it's just across town or to your state capital. God can use it to grow you in your calling to pray. There are things He wants to show you, things you can't learn from just praying from the comfort of your own home.

Prayer journeys, even if they are seldom, are very beneficial for keeping us inspired and focused. There can be all kinds of reasons God will have someone travel to a place to pray. Where are those places for you? Where is God calling you to go and pray? Wherever it is, God will not only use your prayers to bring change, He will also use the journey to change you.

I hope you will believe that God wants you to Pray for Reign. That He can use you as part of His plan to move Heaven to earth, one prayer at a time. As the church and America move forward, they both are going to need prayer warriors who not only know how to pray, but have themselves available to the King of Kings. God is inviting us to join Him in His Holy work of expanding His kingdom. He is looking for us to partner with Him and Pray for Reign.

WORKS CITED

1. The Bible College of Wales. "The Legacy - God's Intercessor." Accessed June 15, 2021. https://www.bcwales.org/legacy

2. Grubb, Norman. *Intercessor*. Ft. Washington: CLC Publications, 2016.

3. Murray, Andrew. *With Christ In the School of Prayer*. Nashville: Billy Graham Evangelistic Association, 1996.

4. Billheimer, Paul E. *Destined for the Throne*. Ada: Bethany House Publishers, 2005.

5. Vocabulary.com. "Definition of Intercede." Accessed July 1, 2021. https://www.vocabulary.com/dictionary/intercede

6. RevivalLibrary.org. "When the Mountains Flowed Down – Duncan Campbell." Accessed August 1, 2021. https://www.revival-library.org/revival_histories/evangelical/twentieth_century/hebrides_revival.shtml

7. Capstone Legacy Foundation. "Dutch Sheets – Synergy of the Ages." Accessed July 15, 2021. https://capstonelegacy.org/synergy-of-the-ages-2/

8. Dobson, James. "Dr. Dobson's Parenting Devotional." Accessed July 31, 2021. https://www.oneplace.com/ministries/family-talk/read/devotionals/daily-devotions-for-parents-by-dr-james-dobson/dr-dobsons-parenting-devotional-apr-9-11658106.html

9. Berger, Steve. "What Does God Have To Do With America Pt. 1." Accessed July 10, 2021. https://steveberger.org/americas-covenant-pt-1/

10. Collins Dictionary. "Definition of Decree." Accessed August 11, 2021. https://www.collinsdictionary.com/dictionary/english/decree

11. National Park Service. "The Reverend Robert Hunt: The First Chaplain at Jamestown." Accessed August 10, 2021. https://www.nps.gov/jame/learn/historyculture/the-reverend-robert-hunt-the-first-chaplain-at-jamestown.htm

12. Berkeley Plantation. "The First Thanksgiving." Accessed June 1 2021. http://www.berkeleyplantation.com/first-thanksgiving.html

13. WordReference.org. "Definition of Beachhead." Accessed August 15, 2021. https://www.wordreference.com/definition/beachhead

14. Biblical Spirituality Press. "Give Me Scotland, Or I Die: John Knox As a Man of Prayer." Accessed July 20th, 2021. https://biblicalspiritualitypress.org/2019/10/22/give-me-scotland-or-i-die-john-knox-as-a-man-of-prayer/

15. Lovering, Daniel. "In 200-year tradition, most Christian missionaries are American." Accessed July 21, 2021. https://www.reuters.com/article/us-missionary-massachusetts/in-200-year-tradition-most-christian-missionaries-are-american-idUSTRE-81J0ZD20120220

16. Christianity.com. "George Mueller, Orphanages Built by Prayer." Accessed July 25th, 2021. https://www.christianity.com/church/church-history/church-history-for-kids/george-mueller-orphanages-built-by-prayer-11634869.html

HOW TO JOIN THE PRAYING FOR REIGN MOVEMENT

I f reading *Praying for Reign* stirred your spirit and made you hunger for more, then you might want to explore the prayer group "Praying for Reign" on social media. This group was founded by the author in 2018 to provide a place for people to pray together online.

This group exists to gather prophetic like-minded believers who feel called to pray for the church, the nation, each other, and anything else that the Spirit of God directs us to pray for.

We are answering the command found throughout God's word to pray, particularly in the current world we live in. Isaiah 62:6-8 references this command when it talks about Jerusalem and the church: "Upon your walls, O Jerusalem, I have posted sentinels: all day and all night they shall never be silent. You who remind the Lord, take no rest, and give Him no rest until He establishes Jerusalem and makes it renowned throughout the earth." We are answering this call and inviting others to join us as we seek His face.

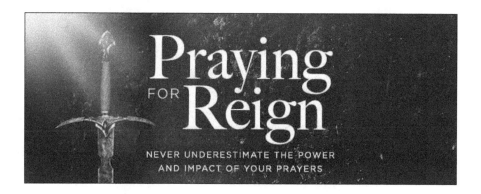

You can become a part the Praying for Reign movement through our private prayer group on Facebook. Please join us in today at www.facebook.com/groups/PrayingforReign.

Looking for ways to connect with the author, Don Newman?

- Connect with Don directly through email at PrayingforReign@gmail.com.
- Follow Don's YouTube channel "Legacy Coach Don Newman" (@CoachDonNewman).
- Follow Don's author page on Facebook at @CoachDonNewman.

CPSIA information can be obtained
at www.ICGtesting.com
Printed in the USA
LVHW031922030223
738627LV00004B/42